BEYOND
/
TU HWNT

Blodeugerdd o Waith gan Ysgrifenwyr Cymreig Byddar ac Anabl
Anthology of Work by Welsh Deaf and Disabled Writers

LUCENT DREAMING

First Edition

Beyond/Tu Hwnt:
Blodeugerdd o Waith gan Ysgrifenwyr Cymreig Byddar ac Anabl
Anthology of Work by Welsh Deaf and Disabled Writers

Published by Lucent Dreaming Ltd.
103 Bute Street, Cardiff, CF10 5AD

Copyright © 2025 Multiple Authors.
The moral right of the authors has been asserted.
All rights reserved. Printed in the United Kingdom by 4edge Ltd.
No part of this book may be reproduced without written
permission from the authors.

Copyright © 2025 Cover artwork by Cerys Knighton.
Edited by Bethany Handley, Megan Angharad Hunter and Sioned Erin Hughes

ISBN 978-1-916632-08-0

CYNGOR LLYFRAU CYMRU
BOOKS COUNCIL of WALES

Lucent Dreaming acknowledges the financial support of
Books Council of Wales and Creative Wales.

To the Welsh Deaf and Disabled community.
/
I'r gymuned Gymreig Fyddar ac Anabl.

BEYOND / TU HWNT

Contents
Cynnwys

Introduction / Rhagymadrodd 1
BETHANY HANDLEY, SIONED ERIN HUGHES AND
MEGAN ANGHARAD HUNTER

State of Bird 7
CAITLIN TINA JONES

The Summers 9
JOSHUA JONES

Garn Fadryn 11
SIONED ERIN HUGHES

One of those radiant people 13
KAITE O'REILLY

[CAPTIONS ON] 19
ED GARLAND

When I say I'm tired 25
BETHANY HANDLEY

Fat/Camp 27
J. BELI FRIEL

Deaf Woman Goes Out To Dinner 33
MAGGIE HAMPTON

Mawl i'r Beirdd Gorweddog 35
IESTYN TYNE

Postcard from the Fish Tank 41
FRAN KIRCHHOLTES

Sometimes the Body 43
LEIGH MANLEY

Shit Superman v The World 45
GREG GLOVER

Ablaeth Rhemp Y Crachach 53
SARA ERDDIG

Car Park 55
JAMIE WOODS

Just Relax 57
KATHERINE WILLIAMS

Juggernaut 63
LENI FRANK

Always 69
GUINEVERE CLARK

Teeth 71
LUCY AUR

ADHD Thing 75
REBECCA WILSON

Masked 79
FREYA F. ELLIOTT

Clinig a Dwy Gacen 81
SIÂN ROBERTS

Recognition 89
SAM SKELTON

Face 91
SAM SKELTON

The Red and White Inhaler 93
GUINEVERE CLARK

Criminal Bodies 95
MATTHEW HAIGH

Grateful 99
DEE MONTAGUE

Untethered 101
PAUL DAVIES

Night Storms 103
LEIGH MANLEY

Dyslexia, Dyspraxia & Desperation: The World of Work 105
DIFFWYS CRIAFOL

Burning Shame 115
RACHEL CARNEY

Dysgu Dargyfeiriol 117
LEE GREEN

Dream* 119
SOFIA BRIZIO

Borderline Questionnaire... 125
ZOË BRIGLEY

Baby-Led Healing 127
KATIE BENNETT-DAVIES

Biographies / Bywgraffiadau.. 133
Acknowledgements / Cydnabyddiaethau................................ 141

Introduction / Rhagymadrodd

BETHANY HANDLEY, MEGAN ANGHARAD HUNTER
AND SIONED ERIN HUGHES

Beyond / Tu Hwnt is a communities-uniting collection of contemporary Welsh Deaf and Disabled voices. By celebrating the diversity and uniqueness of our voices, we aim to fill the void where our stories and experiences always should have existed. Our aim in bringing our poetry, non-fiction and fiction together is to show that our work exists in all its power beyond the barriers and that it always has existed here in Wales. A collection of work by Deaf and Disabled writers shouldn't be radical, yet it is.

Mae croeso i unrhyw un yn y gymuned hon, boed eich amhariad yn weladwy neu beidio. Os cofiwch hynny, bydd eich presenoldeb a'ch cyfraniad tuag at y gymuned yn eich grymuso.

We have had enough of being marginalised and spoken for and over. Welsh Deaf and Disabled voices are still often othered and excluded and it remains challenging to find positive representation of the Deaf and Disabled community. It can be incredibly lonely and isolating to exist as a Disabled person in a world not designed for us, that maintains the barriers that continue to shut us out.

INTRODUCTION / RHAGYMADRODD

The literary community is unfortunately saturated with ableist and audist barriers that make it harder for Deaf and Disabled writers to have our voices recognised. From poor working conditions including unrealistic pay that inevitably hits Deaf and Disabled writers harder, to the expectation that writers have the time, energy and a disregard for their own access requirements to promote their own work, to a lack of Deaf and Disabled editors in the industry, barriers to writing and publication as a Deaf and/or Disabled writer can be exhausting.

Nid yw'r cysylltiadau negyddol gyda'r gair 'Anabl' wedi helpu yn y cyd-destun hwn, chwaith; dwi'n siŵr bod gan bawb gof o glywed y gair 'Anabl' yn cael ei ddefnyddio fel term sarhaus ar iard yr ysgol. Mae'n hen bryd i ni berchnogi'r gair yn falch ac yn ddiymddiheuriad, oherwydd nid gair negyddol mohono, ond term sy'n dynodi ffordd o fod yn ddynol. Mae'r flodeugerdd hon yn ymgais o brofi hynny ar goedd.

The idea for this anthology stemmed from a writing retreat Bethany and Megan held for young Deaf and Disabled writers at the treasured Tŷ Newydd, the National Writing Centre of Wales. Through conversations between Deaf, Disabled and neurodivergent writers, one theme emerged: we did not feel united as a community. One of the biggest barriers to belonging was not identifying as Disabled because they did not feel 'disabled enough'. There's an expectation that a united Disabled community will extend their hospitality to you on acquiring an impairment, declaring 'congratulations, you're now Disabled.' This doesn't happen, nor will an individual automatically gain access to the health and social care and adaptations that they need to have the best quality of life. This is a topic Erin, Megan and Bethany debated in depth upon meeting at Tŷ Newydd. Erin had previously edited the groundbreaking *Byw yn fy Nghroen*, a collection of writing by young Disabled people, and agreed to come on board as an editor.

Cysylltodd sawl cyfrannwr gyda ni cyn anfon eu gwaith yn cwestiynu a oedd eu hanabledd yn eu gwneud yn gymwys ai peidio. Yn arbennig felly, gwelwyd hyn yn achos cyfranwyr gydag anableddau anweladwy neu niwrowahaniaethau. Mae'n hawdd peidio â theimlo'n 'ddigon Anabl' pan fo'r amrywiaeth o brofiadau yn y gymuned mor eang, ond dyna un o'r pethau sy'n gwneud y gymuned Anabl mor arbennig; yr amrywiaeth diddiwedd o brofiadau a ffyrdd o 'fod' yn Anabl sy'n plethu drwyddi, ac mae hynny'n rhywbeth i'w ddathlu.

At the heart of this anthology is pride in our identities and the belief that we are not disabled by our impairments but by the barriers created by an audist and ableist world, as is beautifully explored in Diffwys Criafol's 'Dyslexia, Dyspraxia & Desperation'. According to the social model of disability, disability is the barriers and discrimination perpetuated by our society, not by an individual's impairment. As Matthew Haigh writes in 'Criminal Bodies', 'a world well-designed for [non-disabled people], ill-equipped for [us] awaits.' Since these barriers have been created, they can also be removed. Work throughout this anthology challenges the barriers in innovative, subversive ways from an essay interspersed by captions in Ed Garland's '[CAPTIONS ON]', to Katherine Williams' 'Just Relax' where the scanner's beeps punctuate the poem.

O'r dechrau, roedden ni'n credu'n gryf y dylid cyhoeddi gwaith pob cyfrannwr yn yr iaith wreiddiol yn unig. Mae cyfieithu'n grefft arbennig ac yn allweddol er mwyn creu pontydd rhwng gwahanol gymunedau, ar draws ffiniau ac fel gweithred o solidariaeth. Gall cyfieithiadau llwyddiannus greu rhywbeth o'r newydd. Eto i gyd, wrth wneud hynny, mae'n ffaith anochel ei bod hi'n amhosib cynrychioli'r gwaith heb golli rhywfaint o weledigaeth bardd neu awdur y darn gwreiddiol. Rydym yn sgwennu o safbwynt cymuned sydd wedi'i lleiafrifo trwy gyfrwng iaith sydd wedi'i lleiafrifo, felly mae peidio â chyfieithu hefyd yn weithred wleidyddol herfeiddiol. Rydym yn gwrthod glastwreiddio'r gwaith Cymraeg er mwyn plesio'r mwyafrif, yn union fel yr ydym yn gwrthod glastwreiddio ein balchder o fod yn Anabl er mwyn plesio'r mwyafrif nad ydynt yn Anabl. Gan fod bodolaeth y flodeugerdd ei hun yn weithred wleidyddol o herfeiddiwch yn sgil ablaeth systemig cymdeithas, roedd peidio â chyfieithu'n benderfyniad priodol.

We are proud of the many writers who have shaped this collection, including Sam Skelton, a brilliant writer, who has sadly since passed away and playwright and writer Kaite O'Reilly whose disability arts practices have led the way for Deaf and Disabled writers on the global stage and who has taken Welsh stories to the world. Our work builds on the work of the Deaf and Disabled writers and activists such as Kaite who have enabled our freedom and artistic practice through their tireless subversion of disability stereotypes and a relentless fight for our rights. This anthology is a snapshot of Welsh Deaf and Disabled writers at the time of writing and builds on this foundation of activism, disability arts and Deaf and Disabled pride. *Beyond* asks, united, what's possible?

BEYOND
/
TU HWNT

1

State of Bird

CAITLIN TINA JONES

There were pigeons kissing on the fence yesterday
and I told you this: how their diaphanous plumes
painted God in infinite shape, each clambering
in a muss of feathered innateness. A pigeon does
not evaluate its pigeonness, sum up its state of bird,
or consider if it becomes lesser because it cannot make
a nest. I lined mouldy raspberries in a neat row across
the fence. I watched as they bobbed and teetered to eat
them all, one-by-one splitting open small, seeded bodies.
A beak is a tusk is a tooth, broken in open air. I sucked
raspberry juice from my fingers, curled my nails in on
sugar-wet palms. Something can tilt in the light
and then change: fuchsia flashing emerald then grey,
ebbing neatly, ecstatic, feathered cooing on the forest floor.

1

The Summers

JOSHUA JONES

Spiderman squirting spider-silk from a white, cotton-spun vest /
Girls think the fabulous muscles under my school uniform are real /
A birthday party in soft-play McDonalds / Darth Vader cake /
Hot Wheels arranged by size / plastic dinosaurs / taste of time /
I wished for a brother / Wish fulfilled
/ I used to think all wishes come true /

Uncle and I with matching hair / Does your Mam cut your hair
with the same bowl?/ I wanted to kiss boys and girls /
couldn't kiss either with this shitty haircut / School / a timeloop /
every Parents Evening every report repeated / Your son is bright
/ and gifted / if only we could get him to pay attention!

THE SUMMERS / JOSHUA JONES

Whenever I pay attention to pain / I see white lights and stitches /
The first time feeling / space between socket / bone / pulled apart /
Childhood documented by doctors, slings, casts / stitches /
Was this why I retreated into myself?
/ To allow the body to fix itself? /

The summers of my childhood taste like wild garlic / vinegar /
Chips fall from my paper knees / I bury them in Tenby sand
with my foot / This must be the place /
I felt I could exist somewhere / physically /
I don't wear costumes anymore / No more Spiderman / just
/ Welsh salt / Welsh soil / This skin is a mask /

BEYOND / TU HWNT

Garn Fadryn

SIONED ERIN HUGHES

Ben Garn Fadryn,
fi a'r ci.

Roedd y tir yn tynnu,
fy nhraed yn drybola
o driog du.
Minnau'n gwthio,
yn rhygnu drwyddo
gam wrth gam,
un droed o flaen y llall,
drosodd a throsodd,
dyna chdi,
bron yna,
ac eto...

Mae'r grug bellach
yn fochau afiechyd –
y porffor wedi blino,
ymylon yn brownio.
Eto, mae 'na dlysni,
er nad yw'n iach.

GARN FADRYN / SIONED ERIN HUGHES

Ystyriaf, gwenaf,
a dwi'n gyrru 'mlaen,
y ci a thro llawen
ei chynffon
yn arwain y ffordd.

Dwi'n teimlo'r gwendid
yn curo drwof,
mor gyfarwydd imi
â f'enw fy hun.
Mae'n dwrdio,
strancio,
yn pwyntio bys.
Dwi'n rhoi dwmi yn ei geg
drwy oedi.
Mae'n dofi, yn diolch,
a dwi'n dechrau eto.

Y copa, o'i gyrraedd,
yn teimlo fel dychwelyd.
Dwi'n sbio ar ehangder
fy adra, baneri'r caeau
a môr sy'n brolio'i obeithion.
Mi dala i'r pris am heddiw.
Ond weithiau,
mae ennyd ar ben Garn Fadryn
werth wythnos o orffwys wedyn.

BEYOND / TU HWNT

One of those radiant people

KAITE O'REILLY
from *Something Wonderful, the Beijing 'd' Monologues.*

This is an excerpt from Kaite's international *The 'd' Monologues* – fictional solos written solely for Deaf, Disabled and neurodivergent identifying performers, informed by lived experience. Since 2010 productions have taken place across the UK, South Korea, and Singapore. This is from Kaite's most recent collaboration during lockdown, with Chinese disabled, Deaf and neurodivergent people.

Speaker: When I was a child I believed my body belonged to me completely. Now I feel it's my physical container. Sooner or later I will have to give it back. So until then, I celebrate it and dress it accordingly.

Voice a: *A colourful maxi dress.*

Voice b: *Dr. Martens boots.*

Voice c: *Pyjamas.*

Voice b: *A Tibetan robe.*

Speaker: Clothes: 'Appearance is 30% looks and 70% adornment.' 三分靠长相，七分靠打扮。

Voice a: *A classic black leather jacket.*

Voice b: *A loose-fitting cotton dress that is unrestricted and comfortable.*

Speaker: Ask people what item of clothing their impairment might be, and you'd be surprised by their answers.

Voice c:	*A pure white princess dress, short in the front, trailing at the back. The top like Snow White's, puffy sleeves, bare shoulders.*
Voice a:	*Short rags that don't even cover the skin.*
Voice b:	*A low profile conservative coat but with sexy clothes inside.*
Voice c:	*A Cantonese opera costume.*
Speaker:	Clothes maketh the man and I am self-made: my own creation. People are surprised I dress so well, like they're expecting me to be like a pauper in a period drama – or in one of those flimsy hospital gowns made of paper that don't close at the back... At times it seems my sartorial fabulousness is an affront – someone like me shouldn't look like this, surely? Perhaps they expect me to be in beige, shapeless pull-ons, washed a thousand times and communally used – clothes that are shared, but never owned, like in those institutions where you don't even have your own underwear.

But that's their issue, not mine. Couture isn't just for the non-disabled. I love seeing their jaws drop when I turn up in knocked-off Chanel or Guo Pei – made by myself. I see the designs in magazines or catwalks on social media during Paris Fashion Week and I screenshot, study, and make my own version, adapted and custom-made for my body.

If I meet old neighbours they tell me: 'you look so good!' Well, with my rip-off designer garb of course I do. But I can tell they really mean something else. It's the shock in their faces, tempered with a little fear, like they're meeting a ghost. 'So you're still here? Still holding on?' They expected me to die before adulthood.

'You may not look strong,' my mother said, 'but you're durable. You just dug your heels in and decided to stay despite all the predictions, and you surprised them all.' Which seems to be my natural state – the surprise that dresses spectacularly in bespoke clothes like an Audrey Hepburn or Dilireba. Sometimes I wear jeans and sometimes that cheap synthetic Chinese silk – but never a Cheongsam – not with these hips.

Voice b:	*Body contour elastic dress.*
Voice a:	*A white feather.*
Voice c:	*Hunting clothes.*
Speaker:	'Occasionally,' I joke when talking about my wardrobe, 'occasionally I wear nothing at all, just a dab of perfume behind each ear, like Marilyn Monroe.' And that's frowned upon, too, for people like me aren't supposed to speak like that. We shouldn't be confident, or desirable, but bland and grateful, with a 'thank you' on our lips.

I always seem to create ripples with my panache, which is to be expected, apparently, given my Chinese horoscope – not that I believe in fate, but my mother thinks there's something in it. She said she dreamt of an earthquake the night before I was born and woke the household up screaming of the natural disaster that never arrived – unless, of course, you decide that that describes me.

I prefer 'force of nature'. There's nothing natural about the disaster which befell me. All avoidable. All down to human fallibility and the insufficiencies of resident insurance. Medicine is expensive et cetera et cetera and it's no use dwelling over what could have been. I had a sick body which wasn't given the treatment it needed and so a fixable condition became a permanent impairment. Friends ask if I'm bitter, but there's no style in that. Living and dressing well is the best revenge.

So I taught myself how to sew and how to transform the cheapest of materials into something couture. You can't fake the cut to a beautifully crafted outfit – so what if it's recycled polyester? I get bonus points for being sustainable.

Voice a: *Very tight-fitting clothes made of iron chains.*
Voice b: *A transparent raincoat.*
Voice c: *Something to emulate plants photosynthesizing.*
Speaker: I hate it when people over-compliment me for my dressmaking. Their tributes aren't really based on my skill, but their expectation of what a disabled person can do. My mediocre talent suddenly makes me special and extraordinary, like a dog standing on its back legs and quoting Lu Xun. I wish we could end this binary of ability versus disability and stop excessively praising people with impairments for very small achievements. Let's ban being 'special' and instead allow us all to be ordinary.

But no, we're still set apart – a state to be feared.

I've heard people say they would rather die than become disabled. What nonsense! It's the horror stories and propaganda from TV and the movies that create terror about perfectly natural occurrences.

Voice c: *-A diving suit.*
Voice b: *The nun's black veil, only better designed.*
Voice a: *Very, very thick woollen grey clothes.*
Speaker: My cousin said: 'I expect you'd like to die.' It was a family gathering for Lunar New Year and that was not the kind of chit-chat I was expecting over the longevity noodles. She wanted to know if I was going to commit suicide – and if so, did I need some help? Because she'd understand if I did want to. It would only be normal and expected to want to escape a rubbish body and it would be an

honour, a really cool thing to help me escape the pain and drudgery of my clearly terrible life. And I said I'd think about it, but first I had London Fashion Week and the Jean Paul Gaultier retrospective.

I don't want to die because my body is connected to my soul and it can't exist on its own. I want to push at the boundaries of my existence, meet my limits and exceed them. That's what's driven humankind out of the caves and up onto our back legs and out to explore, to attain, to experience, to learn. Disabled people should be ninjas at this but it's the barriers – both physical and in attitude – that stop us participating and leading the field, surpassing expectations.

Voice c: *Fake fur coat to look like a meow, koala or Yuan bear.*
Voice a: *A long black robe with scales.*
Voice b: *A shackle, a shackle-like garment that binds me. I can perceive the world, but the world cannot perceive me.*
Voice a: *White, reflective, thin, distant, transparent.*
Speaker: With my condition I have to live in the present, but I'm working hard on living in the future – to be reborn from the ashes – one of those radiant people.

[CAPTIONS ON]

ED GARLAND

In Apichatpong Weerasethakul's film *Memoria*, Tilda Swinton plays a woman who hears an intermittent, explosive sound. When she discovers that no one else can hear it, she visits a recording studio and tries to make a young man recreate the sound on a digital audio workstation. She says it's like a large concrete ball inside a metal box immersed in seawater. The captions for the film on the BFI's online player say the sound is [THUD REVERBERATES]. It both troubles and fascinates Tilda Swinton's character, and part of the reason she wants to recreate it is so she can own a simulation that she can access whenever she likes, without having to wait in uneasy hope for the sudden reappearance of the real thing, which is both a sonic event and a psychoacoustic object. After several attempts, the recording engineer produces a half-decent approximation, and Tilda Swinton's character is pleased. The film invites us to contemplate the generative possibilities that arise between language and listening, description and attraction.

[DO YOU SPEAK LITERATURE?]

Tilda Swinton's character writes poetry. Halfway through the film she recites a poem to her sister, who has recovered from an unexpected illness that seemed to be mysteriously related to the intermittent sound. The poem is full of yearning, which suits the film's feeling of subdued persistence: long scenes, camera in a static position or moving slowly, languid dialogue, and a prominent role for [TRAFFIC HUM CONTINUES]. I streamed the film while my internet connection was unstable, and sometimes I couldn't tell whether the film had paused and I was viewing a halted image, or the action was continuing uninterrupted but the actors were staying very still. I don't think Apichatpong Weerasethakul or the BFI intended to make me think about contemporary technological hiccups – the only words I remember from the blurb are 'immersive' and 'botanist' – but the steady flow of images of stillness, within the boundaries of an intermittently frozen laptop screen, pushed my thoughts in that direction. I don't think anyone in *Memoria* had trouble hearing what had been said to them, but when that happens to me, as it often does, I wish I could arrange my features into an expression known as 'buffering face'. It would look like Tilda Swinton sitting yearningly on a bench, and the person who'd just spoken to me would know that I'm taking a couple of seconds to loop their muffled vocals through my short-term memory, hoping for words to emerge from the sounds. In a cinematic analogy of this process, the captions for the scene would end in accurate dialogue, after having begun with [INDISTINCT CHATTER].

[YAK YAK YAK]

Even if you don't watch things with captions enabled, maybe you've noticed this compact, sporty [INDISTINCT CHATTER] caption somewhere before, which has escaped its film and TV origins to become the title, component, or reference point for many other kinds of artistic and cultural production (type it into an image search and behold). A banal ingredient, the opposite of [THUD REVERBERATES], [INDISTINCT CHATTER] does not want to draw any attention to itself. Except when it appears in Greta Gerwig's *Barbie*.

[WE'VE HEARD MORE THAN ENOUGH ABOUT THAT 2-HOUR TOY ADVERT]

One of *Barbie*'s sound designers, Ai-Ling Lee, describes that film's sonic aesthetics as variously 'delightful and otherworldly', 'plastic and pleasant', and 'authentically artificial'. There are no 'real' sounds in Barbie Land. An on-screen bird might be given the sound of a person doing an impression, but never a recording of a live animal. The sound designers also played with stereotypical, ready-made cinematic audio. During the ocean-going section of the 'world travel' montage, for example, there is 'dolphin chatter', which is not just any old recording of a dolphin but the very same recording that occurs in many other films. It's a blunt symbol, signalling to the viewer who can hear it that we are sailing the seas at a cartoonish pace. Thus it supports the 'authentically artificial', rigorously synthetic side of *Barbie*'s sound-world. In this context, a widely used caption like [INDISTINCT CHATTER] has an unusual resonance. Normally, it would seem to simply inform us that none of the people on screen are saying anything distinguishable. In the context of *Barbie*'s sound-world, this bland utilitarian caption trumpets its own aesthetic dimension. As well as providing 'access' to sound, which is still the mainstream idea of what captions are 'supposed' to do for audiovisual media, it participates in the film's explorations of 'plastic and pleasant' audio. In the same way the very popular 'dolphin chatter' sound is delivered with a knowing wink, the very popular [INDISTINCT CHATTER] caption turns up in its party outfit, utilitarian and tipsy.

[HI KEN]

Other good captions in the *Barbie* film were [GLITTER CHIMES], which accompanies the titles' shimmery visual FX, and [ELECTRICAL WARBLE], which comes from a machine, but I can't say exactly which machine because I didn't bother to put that information in my notebook. It's hard to write more than two words in a darkened cinema when you aren't wearing your night-vision goggles. My overall impression was that the captions were slightly more in tune with the sounds and images than is usual in a cinema – not just on the screen but also *in* the film, aligned with the sound designers' creative priorities. They wouldn't be out of place in a Nicki Minaj or Tame Impala song, and the all-caps convention of caption-writing only amplifies their clout.

[COMPUTER WHIRRS]

Another noticeably well-captioned film I've seen recently is Lisa Rovner's *Sisters with Transistors*, a documentary about women who compose electronic music. The captions for the music say things like [BEEPING MERGES INTO A STAGNANT TONE]. Usually, in caption-land, music without vocals is given a single adjective like 'melancholy', or a broad genre label like 'jazz', with little indication of any other characteristics. Sometimes words are abandoned altogether, and all we get is one or two quarter-note symbols. Whoever captioned *Sisters with Transistors* crossed a literary threshold. Their lengthy and evocative, specific and weird approach to caption-writing gives us a glimpse into a future where captions offer more than just 'access'. As many people have been arguing for many years, perhaps most prominently the artist Christine Sun Kim, captions could show us what 'sound is made of. How it moves. Its personality.' But guidelines for caption-writing often state that only sounds deemed 'essential to the plot' should appear in text on the screen; sounds that are essential to a film's aesthetics, atmosphere, tone, and feel – which might be deemed essential by its directors, producers and sound designers and welcomed by its audiences – are deliberately left out. Similarly, computer-generated subtitles on YouTube and other venues render spoken swear words as blank spaces. You can 'access' the exchange of information in a section of dialogue, but the tone and feel — the emotional resonance — is diminished.

[GUIDELINE ADJUSTMENT PARTY]

Of course, there often isn't sufficient time or room to include every word and every sound in every scene. As the writer Benjamin Obler puts it, captioners 'learn to optimise language. Drop the interjections. Keep the meaning. But clip the clutter. It's an art in itself.' Part of the trouble is that judgments of what counts as 'clutter' are often made by hearing people who, by producing captions, decide what aspects of a film or TV show's sound-world D/deaf and hard of hearing viewers will encounter. While working as a captioner, Obler's boss once insisted that he change [SMOOTH POP MUSIC] to [MELLOW POP MUSIC]. It's reassuring to know that some captioners do care about such differences, which influence how we experience the sounds of whatever we're viewing. 'Smooth' has entirely different connotations, and is composed of different tones to 'mellow', and good captioners are sensitive to such distinctions, as literary translators are sensitive to the cultural resonances of words and phrases.

[THE OSCAR FOR BEST CAPTIONS]

I'd like a 'captioned by' credit to appear near the film's name in the listings when I'm considering whether or not to buy a ticket or press play. One I do look out for is the film exhibitor Matchbox Cine, who produce captions that are more aesthetically attentive than most (and which they call 'descriptive subtitles', for solid reasons, but I'm fond of captions' container-ish tone). I'd like to see captions by writers who, in the words of the poet Lisa Robertson, '[resist] the distinction between the essential and the accessory.' The artist Jay Afrisando explores this territory, and a couple of years ago I was lucky to be chosen as one of several captioners for his piece 'In Which to Trust?', a five-channel audiovisual installation presenting viewers with a range of captions for identical scenes. Contemporary poets and novelists are also beginning to reassess what literature can take from audiovisual sonic experiences. Rhys Trimble's *Swansea Automatic* is full of parentheses that sometimes act as captions, which produces a strange faint feeling that you're watching the book as well as reading it. In Sara Baume's *Seven Steeples*, two protagonists whose names are also sounds – Bell and Sigh – are woven into a narrative that pays far more attention to sensory detail, and thus the developments of their physical surroundings, than to the 'action' between them. It feels like a film with extremely acute sound design that slowly dramatises the experience of dwelling, charting the development of a conflict by attending to the physical textures across which that conflict plays out. Its many instances of vivid sonic awareness could teach us how to write better captions, and show us how literary thinking might revitalise those two lines of text at the bottom of our screens.

When I say I'm tired

BETHANY HANDLEY

Rest [*rest*] | the remaining part | the bee in the conservatory seeking nectar from the houseplants | a settling | a wave hesitating on | the beach | an interval of silence | the *oh I'm tired too* | from the writing group | *juggling work and writing is so tiring* | I mean tired as in it took my daily energy to transfer from my bed to my wheelchair | or drag my paralysed legs up the twenty stairs to | bed | rest from old English *league* or *mile* | the distance after which one resets | tired as leatherbacks swimming for one hundred million years | it's a lie they rest retracted into their shells | I'm not talking to non-disabled writers about fatigue again | at rest | the fallen magnolia flowers I gathered as a kid and placed in bowls of water on the table until they bled | away

Enough [*ih*-nuhf] | are you Disabled enough? | as in the man waiting by the blue badge bay to say *this is a Disabled bay* | *they do check blue badges here* | *is it valid?* | he sees my wheelchair with an | *oh* | puts his window back up | sea grass ripped from the seabed by an anchor | the Department for Work and Pensions' fortnightly calls to ask how I've achieved their | goal | *you sat up this week?* | *good* | *you have met your work-related goal* | *you are on track for employment and may receive your* | *£292 for the month* | *but you know you can work lying down?* | dahlias blooming flames before | the frost came | my legs do not need fixing | they are as ornamental as an | orchid's | petals

Adapt [*uh*-dapt] | a young house martin learning to leap into | flight | a biological process of change by which an organism or species becomes better suited | to its environment | ghost pipes growing in dark forests who cannot reach | the sun | have no chlorophyll in their | bodies | yet on they bloom | the adapted car I would wheel into and drive to the top of Blorenge to breathe with the | mountain *oh | wait you don't work or study 12.5 hours a week? | no | writing doesn't count as work | you're not eligible | for a vehicle |* a butterfly fresh from its chrysalis drying out its | wings

Fat/Camp

J. BELI FRIEL

'Fuck you!' Jace yells at the bedroom door, shaking their toes as the pain shoots right to their temples. The door retaliates by swinging back on its hinge, narrowly missing Jace's foot again before they hop to the side. The perfect timing of the backlash would have made them laugh if they hadn't been frantically searching for their jumper. The blue one – light blue, with the cloud patches on the elbows that Ronan had sewed in last October, probably the last time it was washed. Not the navy one, which prickles their skin and clings too tight around the edges of their chest, and is probably due a trip to the charity shop. They pull apart the pile of clothes scattered over the bed, part of some attempt to stand out and wear something different for once, which led them here – late, panicked, and in the same black jeans they had worn for the past week. Soon to be matched with the light blue jumper; the only one that doesn't make them want to pull clumps of flesh off their body and burn them. If they could just find it.

An alarm goes off – something that Diane suggested in their last session, when Jace was complaining about the way time moved slow and fast seemingly without any reason, always leading to them being uncomfortably early or disrespectfully late. The constant explaining had gotten too much – how do people not realise that it's not *respect* that decides whether they arrive on time, but some unknowable whim of the universe dictated only by the speed of the dopamine drip from whatever they're watching online, or the depth of the labyrinth their thoughts have been sucked into? But Diane suggested alarms – which, sure, fine, it *seems* that alarms would help them keep time. One alarm when you have to get ready; one when you have to go; and one when you REALLY have to go.

This is the second alarm.

'Come on – where are you?' Jace mumbles to no one. Their brain scrambles as fast as their hands, retracing every step they made around the– OH!

They run to the bathroom, and there it is – hung over the towel rack, inside-out, having been pulled off during a particularly sweaty you-should-probably-drink-a-glass-of-water kind of bowel movement.

The last alarm goes off as they're pulling their silicone-strapped trainers on, going through the mental checklist. Phone – keys – wallet – mask for the bus – a pen and paper just in case – sunglasses (the winter sun is excruciating these days) – a book for the bus? It all goes in their mini backpack, along with a half-eaten pack of gum left on the kitchen counter. Plus a roll-on lavender oil – just in case the bus stop is particularly smelly.

They check the bus tracker once more on their phone, already sweating in the big winter coat and woolly hat. The bus moved quicker than expected – now three minutes away.

'Crap.' They grab their phone, swinging the backpack over their shoulder while rushing out the door, feeling for the carabiner of keys as the door locks itself behind them. The two staircases feel particularly steep, the rush of adrenaline making them wobblier than usual (which is pretty wobbly). The cold air hits their face; there's no time to double-check everything as the bus pulls into their street and they run with a hand out to stop it.

The bus is nearly empty, with everyone leaving the city for the evening instead of going back in, which allows Jace to catch their breath properly, not worrying about the disgusted or concerned looks of strangers; as if they've never seen a fat person run before. The radio plays an obnoxious talk show, quiet but still too loud, and it's only when they reach for their neck that they realise what's missing – headphones. In a quick panic, they search through the backpack, digging their nails into the corners – no ear plugs either.

'It's fine,' they whisper through deep breaths. 'You're fine.'

They reach to text Diane, stopping to remember the new rules – only emergencies. *'And every panic moment is not an emergency,'* she said with a tone that made them feel like an infant. *'You have the tools now, Jacey, you have to use them.'*

It's not her fault that she's still calling them *Jacey* – that would require Jace actually telling her that it was just 'Jace' now, after they spent all that time explaining why Julia-Claire was now JC (or Jacey). Would Diane even understand that, now, even that has begun to sound like a woman's name, lumped in with the likes of Josie and Macy? It was all moving so fast in their head. Faster than Diane could comprehend. She would never be able to *get it* in the ways she so desperately wanted – and Jace was tired of disappointing people.

There's no long line into the auditorium, despite it being a sold-out show. Only a couple of people laughing with the ushers, chatting as if they know them. They might, in such a small city and such a niche audience for all the *Old Mill* shows, or they might just be doing that thing people seem to know how to do, instantly finding moments of connection without a second thought. One usher spots Jace and gets their ticket scanner ready, clearly hurrying them along. They'd hoped to go to the toilet first, but can't bear the idea of pushing past the line of diligent volunteers, all watching them pick one of only two options.

'Just in time!' the older lady says, smiling at them. She holds her scanner to Jace's phone, and keeps it there while Jace awkwardly searches for the email, wishing they'd thought to pull it up beforehand.

Inside, there are only a couple of aisle seats left. Jace slips into one of them next to a large man wearing a leather vest over an open shirt, chest hair poking through. His forearms extend over the edge of their seat and he moves himself slightly as they sit down, smiling widely to reveal a triple chin covered in stubble. The vest is covered with pins, one that reads *he/him* in the colours of the trans flag, another with Kirby holding a knife, one that's just a butt plug in gold enamel.

The room is full of people whose arms spill over the armrest, whose elbows rest on large stomachs and knees lean against each other, but no one pulls them back into themselves. Here, shoulders move from hunched small to stretched wide, bellies breathe and relax into the full size of themselves. It's impossible to know who is the largest in the room, and for once no one is trying to work out if it's them; it doesn't matter.

After a quick introduction from a short, round queer in dungarees with braids down to their waist, the film starts. A slow, sweeping shot of a dull grey cityscape, accompanied by an acoustic cover of 'I'm Your Man' by Wham! and a typewriter-text reading MAY 1986. Then, in rounded pink letters that are garish against the grey as the camera leads us into a small bookstore, reads FAT/CAMP: A DOCUMENTARY. Jace quietly unzips their bag, searching for a fidget toy – they've forgotten that, too.

The film cuts between interviews with the group of fat queers, now in their sixties and seventies, and the gritty home videos of them laughing, eating, and meeting in 1980s Liverpool. Without subtitles, the words pass through Jace, not stopping to be understood.

Everyone laughs, and they laugh too, out of habit. The film gets louder, or at least seems to, and suddenly there's a fire exit light in the corner, flood lights down the side of the staircase. Everything is brighter, more distracting. The air feels too warm, and Jace realises they didn't take their coat off, still wrapped up in a hat and scarf. The idea of doing it now – the rustling, disruption, heads turning in their direction – is too much. But it's getting warmer, and they can't keep it on. Someone nearby is breathing too loudly, someone else tapping on the wood of their seat. There's a smell – perfume, mixed with sweat, too sweet and sickly. A new headache – they never did drink any water – and the smell reaches the back of their throat; a small wretch. Goosebumps. Teeth grinding. Standing up – quickly, don't look back – faces turning. Light footsteps. Out of the room, doors pushed open. Pacing. Voices.

'Hi, are you okay?'
'Can I help you?'
'Do you need a drink? Some fresh air?'
'Tracey, I don't know– she- he- they're not answering.'
'You okay, hun?'
'Deep breaths'
'Is there someone I can call?'
Then– a person in front of them.
'Hey, come inside, it's quiet.'
They hold open a door. Around them, whispers: *Are you sure? Can you do that?*
They're not answering– how do we–
The person hushes them. Jace enters through the open door, and the person follows, closing it behind them. Inside, there are two sofas, a dressing table, and a small table of snacks.

'You can sit,' the person says, and Jace sits in the middle of the large sofa.

The person is calm and doesn't ask any questions. They search through a bag beside the table, then hand Jace a pair of over-ear headphones. Jace puts them on – calm, the quiet room even quieter now. No more whispers outside or hum of the heating or screeching of cars in the street.

They sit a while in comfortable silence, while the person brings Jace things – a glass of water, a fidget toy, a blanket. Once wrapped up, Jace looks at them properly; they look familiar in a way that doesn't quite fit – like a distant memory or a photograph.

'There's a toilet through there, if you need it,' they say, smiling, as they scroll on their phone.

They do need it, still – only now noticing the heaviness in their lower torso and the tight clenching. They sit on the toilet for several minutes, staring into nothing. As they dry their hands and open the door, someone else is in the room, talking to the other person.

'Five minutes, Alex,' they say, and the person nods at them.

'I have to go,' they say to Jace. 'Q&A time. You want to come? If not, you can stay here, it's no problem.'

Q&A? Then it hits them. The octagonal glasses, the long black hair pulled into a bun with undercut, their round cheeks with the same dimples they'd seen on the posters before they arrived. Not Alex – LX. As in, L.X. Huang, the director of FAT/CAMP.

Jace follows LX out and back into the auditorium, still wearing the headphones, now with sunglasses too, and pushing a marble back and forth in a piece of cloth.

Everyone applauds as LX steps onto the stage, smiling and waving. The host introduces them, and they both sit down opposite each other. LX crosses their legs under themselves, as if at home on their own sofa, and pulls something out of their pocket – a long, colourful piece of plastic, twisted into a rough circle shape, and they twirl it around their fingers while they speak, contorting the shape into new versions of itself.

Jace looks around at the audience – nobody sneers, laughs, or says anything.

Nobody seems to notice. They spot their original seat and return to it, the same man smiling at them; the same kind look in his eyes. He moves his hand to the person next to him, and squeezes theirs. Tightened onto their interlocked fingers are two rings, wrapped in colourful beads that they rub and move in rhythm with LX twisting their tangle toy. The air is still, the room dark; in the quiet, Jace raises their hand.

//
Deaf Woman Goes Out To Dinner

MAGGIE HAMPTON

Here we all are, sitting around a table somewhere posh.
A young person brings food; I smile, *thank you*.
Conversation is everywhere so I act like I'm in
on the chat, nod, smile some more and say, *really?*
But it's mostly pretend; I'm just making the right faces,
watching for clues.

The smiles have gone now, voices lowered,
heads tilted downwards, hiding the words.
I thought I saw *hospital* and *too late*.
Or was it *up the hill* and *two lakes*?
I don't know. Sounds have meshed into a mess.

The mouths move fast, but somehow welded,
like they don't want any sad news to escape.
Look, see how the eyes are loaded, pressed
into shadows. Faces make a terrible chorus,
all of them whispering, *death*.

DEAF WOMAN GOES OUT TO DINNER / MAGGIE HAMPTON

Shall I tap someone on the arm, ask, *what?*
Who? Perhaps I've got it wrong and nobody has died.
Or maybe they will die soon. Dear god.

The young person is back, bringing bread rolls
and fresh air and hope in a small wicker basket.
My face aches. *Thank you.* Spread the butter.
It is something safe to do until heads lift and

talk shifts to the weather or the journey home,
so I can say things like *is it? Oh dear!*
and hope I'm making the right faces.

I taste the bread. Understand it. Wait,
knowing that nothing will ever be the same again.

BEYOND / TU HWNT

Mawl i'r Beirdd Gorweddog

IESTYN TYNE

Neges ar Instagram sy'n fy atgoffa o Siôn Wyn; sgwaryn yn llawn enwau sgwenwyr oedd yn gweithio o'u gwlâu. Mae'r graffig wedi'i godi o restr a gyhoeddwyd yng nghylchgrawn *The Believer* ac mae'n cynnwys y fath fawrion llenyddol llorweddol â Virginia Woolf, Maya Angelou, George Orwell ac Agatha Christie. Sgwenwyr wnaeth hynny o ddewis yw llawer o'r rhai sydd wedi'u cynnwys ar y rhestr. Yr awdures Anabl a niwroamrywiol Esmé Wang sy'n rhannu'r llun, ac mae hi wedi ychwanegu ei henw ei hun ar ben y rhestr wreiddiol. Ar ôl ychwanegu'r postiad at fy Stori innau dwi'n derbyn neges gan gyfaill o fardd o'r Alban, yn diolch i mi am wneud iddi deimlo'n well am dreulio'r penwythnos yn sgwennu o'i gwely.

Y drefn gyfalafol sy'n mynnu mai lle i'r diogyn yw'r gwely yn ystod oriau'r dydd ac yn eironig, yr un drefn sy'n ein porthi gyda'r pethau hawsaf, hygyrchaf, i'n cadw yno – Netflix, Just Eat, y cyfryngau cymdeithasol. Dywedir wrthym na allwn weithio a gweithredu a chreu cymunedau a phrotestio o ganolfan y gobennydd. 'Ma'r byd lawr y lôn, ond ma'r teledu yn y gwely,' meddai Cowbois. Ylwch arnom ni'n pydru rhwng terfynau'r cae sgwâr pan fo'r byd i gyd a'i holl ryfeddodau y tu draw i dro bwlyn y drws; ylwch arnom ni'n cymryd y dewis hawdd.

Mewn ysgrif ar y we, mae Josie Simon yn cyfosod y ffenomen o bydru mewn gwlâu, *bed-rotting*, gyda phroblem lawer ehangach – y modd y caiff gweithwyr eu hecsbloetio nes eu bod yn llosgi allan dan drefn cyfalafiaeth a'r angen am gynhyrchiant ac elw parhaus. Dihangfa rhag byd sydd am ein crwyn yw dianc i gelloedd ein gwlâu. Mae'r athronydd Mark Fisher yn sôn mewn ysgrif o'r enw 'The Privatisation of Stress' am fyd lle mae'r 'gweithle' yn gysyniad niwlog am fod y gweithle yn gyfan oddi mewn i sgriniau ein ffonau symudol; ein cydnabod oll a'n dilynwyr hefyd, fel bod y posibiliad atyniadol o gymryd amser a llonyddwch i wella neu ddygymod yn amhosib. Gallwn gamu allan yn gorfforol ond mae'r sŵn yn ein dilyn o hyd. Ac o ran y gylchred sy'n rhoi i ysgrif Fisher ei henw, y system bydredig sy'n pydru'r gweithiwr, a'r un system sy'n gwerthu'r cyffur i'r gweithiwr hwnnw er mwyn eu cadw wedyn yn eu gwaith, yn rhyw hanner bodoli, yn ddigon da o drwch blewyn i wneud yr hyn sy'n ddisgwyliedig ohonynt cyn mynd adref a methu gwneud dim oll arall.

* * *

Mewn llyfr o 1914 o'r enw *Prif-feirdd Eifionydd* y des i ar draws Siôn Wyn o Eifion gyntaf; cyfrol o hanesion syml nifer o enwogion llenyddol Eifionydd wedi'i hanelu at blant, gyda darluniau o bob bardd ar ddechrau pob adran. 'Mae yn debyg,' meddai awdur y llyfr hwnnw, E. D. Rowlands, 'na ddaeth neb i enwogrwydd llenyddol trwy fwy o anfanteision na Sion Wyn.' Ces afael wedyn ar lyfr cynharach, mwy carpiog a phrin: *Gwaith Barddonol Sion Wyn o Eifion sef John Thomas, Chwilog; yng nghyd a Chofiant o Fywyd yr Awdur*. Ac yn y llyfr hwnnw y gwelais gyntaf ddarlun E. O. Ellis o'r 'Bardd yn ei Wely'. Yn y ddelwedd honno, gorwedda Siôn yn ei wely mewn cell fechan o ystafell – yr ystafell heb fod fawr yn fwy na'r gwely wainsgot ei hun, a'r muriau o'i gwmpas yn orlawn o silffoedd llyfrau llawn. Ar y gwely tua'i ganol mae dyfais i ddal y llyfr sydd ar ei hanner ganddo fel y gall ei ddarllen, ac mae llyfrau eraill yma ac acw ar ben y cwrlid. Ymhellach i lawr y gwely, wrth ei draed, mae hambwrdd bychan ac arno botyn inc a dau gwilsyn yn gorffwys. Gerllaw iddo, yn crogi o'r pared mae rhyw fath o gynwysyddion neu sachau bychain; yn dal rhagor o gwilsynnau efallai, neu bapur i ysgrifennu.

Cafodd Siôn ddwy anffawd yn fachgen ifanc y tybir eu bod wedi cyfrannu at ei gyflwr. Yn naw oed, cafodd ei wasgu y tu ôl i drol pan symudodd y ceffyl yn annisgwyl. Cafodd anafiadau difrifol o ganlyniad. Yna, pan oedd tua phymtheg oed, treuliodd ddiwrnod gaeafol ar lan y môr gyda rhai o'i gyfeillion; yn yr oerfel, clafychodd yn gyflym nes y bu'n rhaid i gyfaill iddo, Emanuel Jones, ei gario'r filltir a hanner yn ôl i Chwilog o'r traeth, ac wedi'r dwymyn a gafodd yn sgil hynny bu mewn rhyw gyflwr o waeledd ar hyd ei oes. Treuliodd ddegawdau yn gaeth i'w wely, a hyd yn oed yn ei gyfnodau iachaf ni allai dreulio mwy na rhai oriau allan ohono.

Un o'r cerddi difyrraf yng nghasgliad Siôn Wyn o Eifion yw'r cywydd mewn 'Diolchgarwch am Anrheg'. Yr anrheg dan sylw oedd *phaeton*, cerbyd bychan olwynog a fyddai'n rhoi rhyddid i'r bardd fynd allan i'r awyr agored pan fyddai'r nerth ganddo i wneud. Mae'n rhaid fod yr emosiwn o gael gweld y byd o'i gwmpas am y tro cyntaf ers dros ugain mlynedd wedi'i lethu'n llwyr. Mewn gweithred o elusengarwch hyfryd, criw o gyfeillion lleol aeth ati i drefnu prynu'r cerbyd, un i'w dynnu gan ferlen ond a oedd wedi'i addasu hefyd i'w dynnu gyda llaw fel y gallai neiaint Siôn a phlant y pentref fynd ag o allan am dro. Mae sôn amdano o'r diwedd yn cael mynd i ymweld â chyfeillion a chydnabod yng Nghlynnog a Phwllheli, ac mewn mannau pellach – Tremadog a Phenrhyndeudraeth. Yn y cywydd, mae'n mynegi'r profiad o weld y byd fel pe bai wedi'i finiogi gan bob synnwyr:

Erfyniaf drwy Eifionydd
Gael rhoi tro i deithio'r dydd,
A gweled bröydd gwiwlwys
O fewn i wlad Arfon lwys;
Dyffryn tirion Meirionydd,
A Lleyn deg, llawen y dydd!

Caf fy atgoffa o'r llawenydd yn llinellau Siôn Wyn wrth weld cydnabod ar y we yn rhannu diléit y troeon cyntaf allan ar y llwybrau gwledig, caregog sydd mor annwyl iddi yn dilyn dod yn ddefnyddiwr cadair olwyn llawn-amser.

> Heb wegi mi debygwn,
> Cerbyd haf harddaf yw hwn...

Yr hyn y deuir yn ôl ato ym mhob disgrifiad o Siôn yw rhinweddau ei gymeriad; tynerwch ei gydwybod, ei raslonder a'i allu i sgwrsio'n rhwydd gyda phlant bach ac ysgolheigion uchel-ael fel ei gilydd. Ceir yr argraff ei fod yn astud a chraff wrth adnabod rhinweddau pobl eraill hefyd; ac yn fwy na dim yn gymeriad diymhongar a diolchgar, a ryfeddai'n blentynnaidd at ryfeddodau ei fyd. Er cyfynged ei orwelion daearyddol, roedd dyfnder i bopeth arall yn ei gylch.

* * *

Mae fy nghyflwr i fy hun yn un nad oedd triniaeth iddo tan ryw ganrif yn ôl. Cyn darganfod inswlin ym 1921, dedfryd o farwolaeth, a honno'n un fuan, oedd diagnosis diabetes math 1. Mae hanes Leonard Thompson yn enwog erbyn hyn; y bachgen 14 oed o Toronto oedd yn marw o'r cyflwr yn derbyn, fis Ionawr 1922, y chwistrelliad inswlin cyntaf erioed a'r glwcos yn ei waed yn syrthio o fewn 24 awr i'r lefel arferol. Cydnabuwyd gwaith Frederick Banting, John Macleod, J. B. Collip a Charles Best gyda'r Wobr Nobel mewn Meddygaeth ym 1923.

O ddydd i ddydd, gallaf gymryd y cyffur sy'n fy nghadw'n fyw yn ganiataol. Diolch i'n Gwasanaeth Iechyd Gwladol, nid wyf yn talu ceiniog amdano chwaith. Ond mae'r Gwasanaeth Iechyd dan fygythiad; mae'i systemau'n ddiffygiol, neu mae ganddo ddiffyg systemau. Erydir fesul esgus yr hyn y gallwn ei ddisgwyl ganddo. Fe'i collwn yn hwyr neu'n hwyrach, os pery pethau i symud i'r un cyfeiriad. Weithiau, yn ddiweddar, aeth y system bresgripsiynu yn dyllog; bu pecynnau'n mynd ar goll neu waeth, yn peidio cyrraedd o gwbl. Prinder mewn nwyddau, prinder pobl. Prinder malio, efallai. Ar yr un pryd, diolch i algorithmau'r we, rydw i'n agor Facebook ac yn cael fy nhargedu gyda hysbysebion am yr union offer a ddefnyddiaf i fesur lefelau glwcos fy ngwaed, ar werth am grocbris fel datrysiad *wellness* gyda rhesiad o selébs i'w hysbysebu. 'I started using ZOE. I want to live a longer and healthier life,' meddai seren *Dragons' Den*, Steven Bartlett wrth y camera, y brandio melyn zen yn tywynnu a'r synhwyrydd bach ar ei fraich, yr union declyn hwnnw yr arferwn ei weld ar freichiau eraill – mewn pyllau nofio ac ar y bws ac wrth aros am fy nhecawê – a gallu cychwyn sgwrs a theimlo undod dros y profiad a rannwyd gennym. 'This tiny device has changed the way I eat breakfast, *every* day', meddai rhywun enwog arall, nad ydw i'n ei adnabod.

Ar un wedd, rydw i'n cywilyddio at yr hunanoldeb dwi'n ei deimlo ynghylch y cyflwr meddygol sydd gen i; y synwyryddion oedd yn ein gosod ni ar wahân, ac fe'n cyflyrwyd cyhyd i gredu mai yr hyn a'n gwnâi yn wahanol oedd ein gwendid. Roeddwn i – ac mae'r diolch am hyn yn fwy nag unrhyw beth arall i'r weithred o ysgrifennu am y profiad – wedi dechrau hawlio'r labeli a roddwyd arnaf fel pethau i fod yn agored, yn *falch*, yn eu cylch; ac roedd y cylchoedd bach plastig ar fraich yn ymgorfforiad o hynny. Preifateiddiwyd fy mraint fach arbennig i; rhoed pris ar fy salwch innau.

* * *

Mae byw yn ein byd ni yn her unigryw, a dyna'r gair. Tueddaf i wingo braidd pan roddir heddiw yn y glorian yn erbyn adegau eraill yn ein hanes; y gwir mewn difrif yw nad oes posib cymharu o gwbl. Nid yw'r rhai sy'n ein galw'n genhedlaeth groendenau, neu yn mynnu fod cenedlaethau eraill wedi'i chael hi'n waeth fel pe byddai hynny yn rhyw anrhydedd mawr, yn ychwanegu dim o ddefnydd ymarferol i'r drafodaeth. Weithiau does dim i'w wneud ond encilio; a hynny o ba bynnag reidrwydd sy'n ein gyrru yno.

Molaf y sgwennu o'r gwely, y sgwennu sy'n digwydd pan nad oes llawer o ddim arall i'w wneud. Molaf y man unigryw y mae salwch yn achosi i ni sgwennu ohono. Molaf y brotest sydd ymhlyg yn y weithred o gau'r llenni a chodi'r dwfe am ein clustiau. Molaf y dybiaeth o ddiogi, o wendid a chlafychiaeth; y gochl a'r amser rydd y pethau hyn inni newid ein hunain a newid y byd. Molaf, weithiau, yr esgus fach ychwanegol sydd gennyf fi.

Postcard from the Fish Tank

FRAN KIRCHHOLTES

in your aquarium, you expect to see
quiet boys obsessed with planes or cars or quantum physics
young men who hardly speak and refuse to meet your eyes
old, grumpy men that have always eaten the same dinner
and worn the same cut, fabric and colour shirt for 40 years

but I'm in here too
compiling food allergies like Bingo points
way too trusting, way too literal
unable to accept that my body grew hips and breasts
when in doubt – smile!

my favourite place is the cave
so I can hide when it's all too much
like when you buy a different brand of food
or when cleaning the tank upends my routine

POSTCARD FROM THE FISH TANK / FRAN KIRCHHOLTES

some days my scales itch and I wonder how easy living
outside the water must be
no scales
no special adjustments just so I can function
always out in the open
never on display

Sometimes the Body

LEIGH MANLEY

Sometimes the body falls behind, slow-turns sick lightning quick.
Sometimes the body survives. Sometimes the body falls in its prime,
trips a switch to call time; sometimes fails on the starting line.

Sometimes the body falters for no apparent reason, sometimes
drifts as snowfall out of season. Sometimes the body fits.
Sometimes the body puzzles. Sometimes the body fights. Sometimes

the body struggles. Sometimes conserves energy with a dimming
of the light. Sometimes yearns for catch-up in this game of equal rights.
Sometimes the body rests. Sometimes the body recovers. Sometimes

the body grieves an old friend being smothered. Sometimes the body
shapes to defy orders as well as odds; sometimes shakes a fist
at medicine, surgeons playing gods. Sometimes the body rocks.

Sometimes the body streams. Sometimes the body checks its wealth
before the sharpness feeds. Sometimes the body curls. Sometimes
the body crawls. Sometimes the body worships the body's mass

of flaws. Sometimes the body speaks up, promises not to die.
Sometimes the body asks itself why it was sold a lie. Sometimes
the body falls behind for a second time.

Sometimes the body battles. Sometimes the body
pines. Sometimes the body blossoms.
Sometimes, sometimes, sometimes.

Shit Superman v The World

GREG GLOVER

Your memories are malleable, they change every time you revisit them as you sculpt, mould and reshape them until they give you exactly what you want, what you need, which if it's your first memory is somewhere between warm and fuzzy, but not mine. Mine is cold and hard and never changes, taking place in a white room, with a man in a white coat who looks like a rat as he says…

'something, something, meningitis…'
'something, something, nearly died…'
'something, something, with the result that your left ear is now dead.'
'And my right?'
'Not quite.'

And with that I was ushered into a strange netherworld where everything
fizzed
crackled
and popped

and was sometimes really loud but then other times really quiet like I was underwater with lots of whooshing and gurgling and then an echo, which meant that I looked constantly surprised, which seemed to annoy my Granch who announced, 'I think the boy's twp.' My parents not disagreeing as not one photograph exists of me between the ages of five and eleven.

Not even the school photo and everyone bought that and school was...

It was okay to start with because all we did was just run around the yard going 'aaaaaaaargh' saying, 'I dare you to lick that snail' or 'stick that button up your nose.' Pretending to be Superman because Superman was the best because he could fly and shoot lasers out of his eyes but was 'far too violent', so we all had to 'play nicely'. Counting down the minutes before we could all bomb up the woods to shout, scream, smash sticks, lob bricks and build traps for all the monsters who no one ever saw but were definitely there, watching, waiting for just the right moment to drag us away, never to be seen again.

But then, aged nine EVERYTHING changed as now EVERYONE noticed EVERYTHING all the time because even though I did what they did, laughed when they did, it was always that second too slow, too fast, which meant getting called 'deafo, deaf bastard, deaf twat, deaf Vader...

DEAFACATOR.'

Kyle grinning. Knowing that this was THE ONE that contained just the right mix of humour and humiliation and meant that I always had a stomach ache or a headache and was just a complete ball-ache according to my dad who wanted 'this shit sorting now' and dragging me up the hospital where they gave me something 'that will totally revolutionise the way you interact with people' but just made everything about a million times worse because now I had a hearing aid, which was connected to a transistor that sat in the middle of my chest in a harness.

In a fucking harness, which my mam said made me look really cool, like a superhero, like Superman.

It didn't.

It just made everyone sound like a Dalek, which was pretty fucking scary with everyone shouting, 'Deafacator, Deafacator' into the box in the middle of my chest. My head about to explode until Kyle said, 'You know what I think...' as everyone stopped. Me thinking, no, no, no, no, please god no because he had that look in his eye, the one that made me want to run head first into a wall so I wasn't conscious for whatever he was going to say next...

'I think he looks like a shit Superman.'

And that was it.

Everyone started shouting...

'Is it a bird?'
'Is it a plane?'
'No, it's Shit Superman!'

Mam telling me to ignore them.
Dad saying, 'You need to stand up to them.'

Which is bollocks, total crap that only ever works in films when in the real world they arrange ...mediation.

Which was just lots and lots of talking and saying how we were feeling, which was really fucking scared because even though I could hardly hear what the teacher was saying I could see Kyle's eyes had begun to narrow as his lips began to purse meaning that I was going to have to run all the way home and not just today but tomorrow and the day after that, until it was the summer holidays when the highlight of my day would be to see how long I could hold my shit in for, before going to bed in the middle of the afternoon with all my clothes on, feeling just so…

'Aaaaaaaaaaaaaaaaaaaaaaaaaargh.'

… twisting my ears until I had to stop because it really hurt and then just lying there staring up at my ceiling as I followed the Aertex swirls round and round on an endless loop. Not thinking anything. My mind a complete blank. And then nearly jumping out of my skin as my mam touched my shoulder going, 'Your friends are outside.'

'My what…?'

'Kyle…'

And even though I was boiling hot I felt my insides go freezing cold while at the same time I was sweating, my scalp tingling, just rambling, words pouring out of me…

'I don't feel very well. I feel a bit sick. I've got a headache. My foot hurts. I don't think I can walk…'

But she just stood there, arms folded because this was not up for discussion. And standing there at the door was Kyle with two bigger boys saying, 'D'you wanna come up the woods?' And Mam saying, 'Of course he does.' And shutting the door behind me. And I've never felt quite so alone, my legs like lead. Knowing that whatever this was, was probably going to hurt but also be quite demeaning and be something that I'd look back on in years to come with a burning sense of guilt and shame that I didn't try and stop them, when in reality there was nothing I could do as there seemed to be a certain inevitability about it all. Like it had been preordained by some higher power.

And each time I thought... now.
They're going to turn around... now.

They didn't. Not even when we reached the first trees, just going further and further into the woods as I turned around taking one last look at my house thinking

maybe
I
could
just

but I couldn't because that is when they do actually turn around. Kyle now seemingly relegated to just lurking on the side as the other two pick up some really quite thick... not sticks, more like branches and as I go to do the same, the one with the bowl cut says, 'not you' and 'gis it here' and wrestles the harness and transistor off me, putting it on saying, 'I'm Superman' and 'move.'

And as we moved I realised that I wasn't panicking. That I actually felt quite calm because even though I could hear the boys shouting I couldn't make out the actual words above all the fizzing and the popping which removed all the threat and didn't seem to be at all connected to the branches jabbing me in my back, which allowed me to take in my surroundings. And even though it was really dark, almost black in certain places, I noticed that the wood seemed to be alive as shapes and shadows flitted in between the trees, sometimes quite close to the ground but then other times higher up, looking quite solid, looking like...

But that must've just been the light.

And then it's time as they spin me round to face them but they don't seem very happy. They actually seem quite distracted, looking first this way, then that and looking quite scared but then looking at me again and remembering what they've come here to do. Grinning at the muscle memory of all the previous times they've reached this exact point in the proceedings.

The best bit.

Better than the actual hitting, slapping, punching. The bit where they explain what they're going to do as they linger over each tiny detail, especially the words

cut
slice
stab

as they discard their branches and produce a knife. No words necessary now as they pass it from one to the other, slicing the air in front of them like they're going to cast a spell. Almost dancing but then stopping, backing away as they point first left, then right and then up, down, almost to the ground as Kyle slips away.

Which is greeted by a full 360 degree turn by Not Bowl Cut while Bowl Cut advances on me, saying in a voice that skips past the fizzing and the popping, 'I am going to cut you,' which momentarily drags me back into the scene but not for long as he wheels round to see his friend running back the way we came.

And for a split second I think he's going to do the same but then he catches my eye and knows he can't do it as he holds the knife in front of him, willing me away, tugging at the harness but that takes two hands to undo as I slowly, quite deliberately take a step towards him

and then another

Which doesn't compute. This shouldn't be happening as he drops the knife, just wanting the harness gone but he's all fingers and thumbs when you need to lift and pull but it's all too much. His eyes darting everywhere like they've lost their moorings, whilst I'm cocooned in a fuzzy ball of whizzing and whooshing until finally he's free and runs off but not the way we came but into the darker bit. The bit where there seems to be the most movement.

* * *

And playing on the school yard early one September morning I notice that wherever I am Kyle isn't and if I ever do get too close to him he very quickly needs the toilet or goes to stand by the teacher as I start to follow him round the yard chanting…

'Is it a bird?'
'Is it a plane?'
'No, it's Superman!'

Before bombing off, arm outstretched, coat flying behind me, doing the music.

BEYOND / TU HWNT

Ablaeth Rhemp Y Crachach

SARA ERDDIG

'Mae'n cymryd blynyddoedd
i astudio'r grefft o farddoni,' medda hi;
O! yr eironi. Achos dyna be' dwi
'di bod yn ei wneud, 'sti,
ers o'n i'n ryw *seventeen*...
yn barddoni mewn *bedsits* efo beiro!

Do tad, mi es i'r steddfodau bach lleol,
a'r un fawr genedlaethol, hefyd;
cyfrannu, barddoni, 'sgrifennu, cymdeithasu –
yn fwy nag eraill o fro fy mebyd.

Ond mae'r sin lenyddol Gymraeg yn seiliedig
ar egwyddorion a meddylfryd niwrotypigal,
sy'n fy eithrio o bob cornel.

'Diffyg llythrennedd', yr unig adborth ges i,
a hynny ddim yn helpu o gwbl, gan mai
nam yr ymennydd sy'n achosi hynny.
Mae angen cymorth, cefnogaeth, a dealltwriaeth,
er mwyn cynnwys ein hamrywiaeth
yn stori fawr gwilt clytwaith 'Y Cymry'.

ABLAETH RHEMP Y CRACHACH / SARA ERDDIG

Chi'n cydnabod yr angen am gydraddoldeb,
ac amrywiaeth i raddau, ond nid anabledd o gwbl;
well peidio sôn am hwnnw – achos, onid diffyg ymdrech
'di hwnnw, wedi'r cyfan, yn y bôn?

Mae'r bwlch rhwng ein bydoedd mor eang,
fel bysa angen rhyw fath o wyrth
i dy helpu di i weld fy nhalent o gwbl:
YR HOLL BWYNT YW FY NGWAHANIAETH!

Mae 'teilyngdod barddol' arferol yn rhywbeth rhiniol
ac yn ddirgelwch yn ei gynildeb amwys;
mae 'na fwy nag un ffor' o fod yn fardd, 'sti!

Ond dene fo, dim ots... dim pwynt dadlau.
A' i ymlaen i chwarae yng nghae eang, braf y byd,
y tu hwnt i dy gilfach gul, ddiddychymyg di,
lle mae popeth mor undonog.

Wedi fy sbarduno, gan aildanio'r tân yn fy mol
a'r creadigrwydd yn llifo drwydda i,
a' i ati o ddifri, yn ffyrnig, ddi-baid,
i rannu barddoniaeth am fy enaid
hynod, od, i.

Car Park

JAMIE WOODS

It was one of those tight car parks
too small for a busy beach
we tailed a Volvo snaking through it
until they found a space
the only space
we stopped as they started to manoeuvre
until they realised it was a disabled space
you could see them pause
as they considered it for a second or two
then awkwardly turned
three-pointedly and drove back past us
staring into our car
passing judgement
as we pulled in and parked
sucks to be you
I thought
as I strapped up my poisoned knees
and placed my blue badge on the dashboard
still fatigued from yesterday
from last year
since forever

I

Just Relax

KATHERINE WILLIAMS

'Just relax,'
        says the technician
as I lower myself into the tube
'Have you had one of these before?'
I scoff.

I know now to avoid any metal fittings on my clothes
no jewellery
        no zips
                no buttons
                        no bra clips, not even loops of a non-wired
                        bralette
Have I had one of these before? Hah.

My things-containing-metal are safely stashed in a hospital locker.
    keys   phone   money

He flicks a switch and the room starts to hum
The locker key on its numbered keyring flies out of my hand and hits
the wall with a clang

JUST RELAX / KATHERINE WILLIAMS

Balls.

Even seasoned veterans are fallible, I guess.

'Okay Mrs P, I'm starting the scan now.
Lie back and keep still.
just relax.'

                    [**pause**]

	clang
'On the M5 there's congestion around Avonmouth.'	**clang**
	clang
The radio I asked for is kind of annoying	**clang**
I've got an emergency buzzer	**clang**
'Just press the button if you have a problem,	
you'll be able to talk to me.'	**clang**
This is an emergency, right?	**clang**
The music is bugging me, please change it.	**clang**
	clang
NO.	**clang**
Don't be that person.	**clang**
Health workers are highly skilled professionals.	**clang**
He's doing a Very Important Job.	**clang**
Did we learn nothing from the clapping?	**clang**

                    [**pause**]

BEEEEEEEP BEEP BEEP BEEP BEEP BEEP BEEP BEEP BEEP BEEP BEEP BEEP BEEP

The kind of person
that would ask a health worker
to change the music in an MRI scanner
is a bad person.
I'm glad I'm not that kind of person.

[pause]

I've got my priorities right.
Close call though.

boom	I can feel this as much as I can hear it
boom	lowermost furthest left part of the tube
boom	I am reminded of Red Dwarf
boom	The Cat, hooked up to all sorts of machines
boom	goes the bass drum *heart rate monitor*
boom	tssssh de de, tssssh de de, tssssh de de high-hat *blood pressure*
boom	dink dink dink tom-tom rim shots *some other health thing*

Twenty minutes it takes.
Surely it's been at least eight.
I could count it.
Shall I count it?

One (alligator)
    two (alligator)
        three (alligator)
            four (alligator)
                five (alligator)

JUST RELAX / KATHERINE WILLIAMS

whirr
whirr
whirr
whirr
whirr

Can't even keep a train of thought going in here.
I wonder if he can tell.
Modern technology is amazing.
He probably knows my mind is jumping all over the place.
Does this mean I'm not doing well at this test?
Am I failing an exam I didn't know I was taking?
Oh God.
I wish I was better at this.
Can you train yourself to corral your thoughts?
Shit.

What is he actually doing up there in that booth?
Surely it's all computerised these days.

[pause]

Maybe I should retrain as a radiographer.	**beep**
Is he a radiographer?	**beep**
could give something back.	**beep**
I bet the pay is pretty good.	**beep**
I'll just make a voi—*scheisse*, phone's in the locker.	**beep**
This outfit doesn't even have pockets.	**beep**

[pause]

CLUNK

Jack should be having his dinner now.

CLUNK

It'll be better for him to eat now, keep his routine.

CLUNK

Bedtime will be easier.

CLUNK

It'd be nice if they could wait for me though. I won't be long. It must have been fifteen minutes now. Or maybe ten. Time is weird. Was it definitely eight minutes before or did I dream that?

CLUNK

We can eat together.

CLUNK

Instil good habits, table manners, and a respect for food. It's what all the baby books say.

[pause]

'Are you alright in there? You've been ever so good.'

GOOD.
I am a middle-aged professional.
Wife and mother.
FFS.

The bed bit of the tube slides out into the open air.
I blink in the overhead lights.
Slowly,
   creakily,
      I sit up

Swing my legs off the bed and stand.

I look at the man behind the glass, the focus of my thoughts for so long.
He waves.
'You're all done.
                We got a very clear image.
                              Nice one.'

So I did ok on the test? Kept my brain still?

He continues
'The consultant will interpret this for you. It's not my job to do that.'

The thought I've been avoiding sears into my brain like a red-hot poker
Or, indeed, like whatever might be lurking.
Why am I here?
What's wrong with me?

                                                Relax, indeed.

Juggernaut

LENI FRANK

Last night while we were out for dinner, I told my sister I was autistic. I hadn't planned to, but we were reminiscing about our miserable childhood. Two anxious, perimenopausal inadequates, trying to drink enough wine to force ourselves to laugh about those awful years. She asked what was the point of a diagnosis at my age, what difference could it make. I couldn't think of an answer that night, which might have been the wine, but the question kept buzzing round my head.

Autism was an unfamiliar word in our family until my daughter was referred for a diagnosis during primary school. The staff noticed behaviours which we thought were parts of our daughter's personality: endearing little quirks that made us smile, but in class these were causing disruptions. We were confused and asked what the teacher thought the issue was, and she cast her eyes down guiltily, refusing to look at our faces. From her demeanour I thought it was going to be another complaint about not listening and raised my chin defiantly but no, an unexpected word came out of her lips like blasphemy, breathy and forbidden – suspicions of '*autism*'. It took four years to get the diagnosis. I tried to learn everything about the unfamiliar word and very familiar behaviours.

The similarities between myself and my daughter were too strong, more than just familial links, and the feuds I fought for her I recognised as things I'd swallowed down in bitter pills myself over the years. I was vicariously fighting battles I wished had been fought for me, and I didn't want her to be forced to swallow. Thoughts of my own autism were whispers, silent ghosts moving opaquely through my head, and we studiously ignored each other as we passed in corridors.

Life got harder as my children got older, and in my forties a fog of low mood rose from under my feet. I was tired all the time and found people harder to tolerate, I was increasingly isolated and became self-employed so I could work at home on my own as I couldn't cope in busy offices. If I had to go out, I would drink to encourage my uptight nerves to loosen enough to survive the evening. Certain sounds would make me want to rip off my own ears rather than abide another minute with a noisy crisp eater, tea slurper or gum chewer, let alone the overpowering smell of perfumes and aftershaves. Voices and thoughts pushed themselves like unwanted visitors into my mind, taking over the sofas and changing the TV channels.

My husband said I hid in my writing, which was true – writing calmed me and shut out the multitude of noisy thoughts and allowed me to concentrate on one thing. Painting words into sentences and paragraphs was meditative and I immersed myself in the peace it brought, but I had to scrape time off the day to accommodate it. I would wait impatiently until everyone had gone to bed then sit down at 11pm until the early hours, sometimes getting up again at 5am to write just a bit more and take longer lunch breaks to get my fix. I'd make notes on walks or in the middle of conversations, snatching five minutes here and there to read through what I'd written the night before to gain scraps of comfort. I was guilty of stealing slivers of time for myself, but couldn't stop doing it.

I met another autistic mother and we became first acquaintances, then dearest friends. I felt my chest loosen, my diaphragm deepen, my stomach unclench. I felt safe in this newfound sisterhood, but it's taken a lifetime to feel this way. I can be myself, however dark, introspective, or joyous that is, and I will be forever grateful for the acceptance and understanding, the love, the feeling of 'not being too much'. In the past, friendships had depleted me and made me question myself. I'd said things that made people uncomfortable, I'd been ghosted, avoided, whispered about, laughed at. I'd lie to fit in the wrong shaped boxes and put myself in situations that caused me physical pain and terrified me, rather than saying no. I'd not been honest with myself or others a thousand times over and I'd mask and mask and mask until I could no longer recognise myself in the mirror. But at nearly fifty, I learned that friendships with the right people never felt wrong. We build each other up, we're consistently kind and most of all, it never feels like hard work.

Did she mention it first or did I? I can't remember who, but it was already there like a cold current swirling round our ankles, that unspoken question, and I eventually put my friend on the spot.

'Do you think I'm autistic?'

Her beautifully constructed, careful answer, 'I think you have many autistic traits.'

The whispers got louder, the ghosts solidified and put their visible vertebrae into haunting me. Once I started asking the questions, I had to know the answer. Who am I? What am I? Why am I like this? I went to see my GP about something completely different, and as I was about to stand and leave I froze, unable to move, and the doctor looked at me with concern.

'Was there anything else?'

'I think I might be autistic.' I hadn't planned to say it, but couldn't hold it in.

She listened with kind eyes, then referred me for a diagnosis and warned that it might take years, but by then my head was a buzzing wasp nest. I couldn't sleep and it was driving me mad. I felt lost and didn't know which team I was on, stuck floating in some strange limbo, a burden to my loved ones with my ricocheting emotions and self-doubt. Intrusive thoughts and voices crescendoed and to retain my peace of mind, I referred myself to a private clinic for an assessment.

My husband was unhappy, and we lived in booming silences as I was no longer the person I once was, the person he knew and loved. I asked him about my 'skills and strengths' as part of the pre-assessment. In a brief email he answered, *'She is persistent, has endurance and has never neglected our children. She is very competent at her work whatever that has been and always polite in all spheres.'*

I am water; I have no colour, taste or shape.

On the day of the assessment, I was terrified I was making myself appear more autistic. I couldn't remember who I was because I'd been so many different people for so long, and I couldn't remember me. At the end of the meeting I was asked what difference a diagnosis would mean, and I wanted to weep. I needed to know if I was autistic or not, I wanted the truth, and of course I was.

I was warned it would get harder before it got better, I remember that bit. I remember being told to seek out the things that bring me joy and to avoid the things that took joy away. A symmetric Venn diagram to make sense of myself. Round and simple. Everything else from that day is a blur.

I told my husband, my friend, then life carried on, but I was in freefall and the world below disappeared. There is little support for adults post-diagnosis and I'm still tumbling. My husband told me not to tell my children because of the effect it would have on them. So I am, but still I'm not. I'm still in disguise in a neurotypical world, choosing which head to put on like Worzel Gummidge. Who do you want me to be today?

Once I received the full report, I felt sadness; a desperate, unshakable sadness at the words in front of me. I was sad for the child I'd been, growing up without understanding my oddness. I wanted to go back and hold her tight, to whisper a promise that one day it's going to be okay; it's the world, not you. You're lovely, imaginative and funny, and you will brighten lives. If that child was a houseplant, I'd put her wilting frame on a different windowsill with less sun.

The things I disliked were harder to tolerate. Now that I understood, I had sympathy for myself. I couldn't scrape my soft insides raw and I became kinder towards myself, treating my discomforts as valid. Having found threads of my authentic self, I couldn't stop being more me. My muchness was expanding, the layers of otherness were shedding like snake skin that I couldn't stick back on, and beautiful bright scales lay beneath.

I'm not without doubt, and nasal voices constantly question the diagnosis: did you fake this? Did you pick the autistic head to wear that day? Did you exaggerate? Did you want the attention? I ask myself am I autistic *enough* to call myself autistic, and it's a description I'm still struggling to confidently claim for myself. I try to gently tell myself I don't need a second or a third opinion, and it's okay to ask for help or for adjustments to be made.

I read, and there are understanding voices within spines and covers that make me feel less alone. Poetry is a balm for my soul and creates a beautiful place to soothe my mind. I carry noise cancelling headphones everywhere to shut out the noisy world, and when tiredness hangs around me in a dark miasma, I no longer have the fight to rage against it. In the past when I'd taken to bed for days, we laughed about me being lazy, but now I know I'm burning out. We don't laugh anymore.

My marriage has become harder, and I can't find a mask that fits or a smile left to plaster on. On average, an autistic person dies sixteen years earlier than a neurotypical person. On that basis I have about seventeen years left. Seventeen precious years. I can't bear the loudness, the atmospheres, the loneliness. My anxiety levels are worse than ever, but perhaps it's to do with impending seismic changes and the distant rumble of thunder (it's going to get worse before it gets better, repeat ad infinitum until it is).

Back to the original question of why I chose to get an autism diagnosis just before I'm fifty and the difference it could make. Knowledge of my autism is the juggernaut overthrowing everything inauthentic in its path, changing how I view the world and forcing me to adjust. During these early days I am a wild scribble of emotions, but there is comfort in understanding and knowing I'm not alone, and the support from my tribe has been huge.

I've never felt that I have a disorder and I don't want to call it that. I love my creative, noisy mind even on days when it feels like a child sitting behind me, kicking the back of my chair, whispering 'there's still time to write a thousand words' on Christmas Day, or throwing Mentos into the glass of Cola I'm trying to sip. Occasionally, glimmers of joy appear and I make sure that's the direction I follow, letting them light the path like fireflies to kinder, quieter days where it really will be okay.

BEYOND / TU HWNT

Always

GUINEVERE CLARK

   Hooked over the pram
or gazing in your direction. I
sit nestled against a stranger by the toilets.

   My arms, released from labour
for a while. You glide – carriage in carriage –
softly jolted, coast to coast.

   From Grimsby to Swansea, I'm
congratulated on your silence,
given half-smiles, nods, birth stories,

   someone's cardigan for a curtain
from the light, as
motherhood is always a performance.

1

Teeth

LUCY AUR

I

<u>Counting teeth</u>

When a tooth is missing you need not run your tongue over the gap to know it is not there.
     I count my teeth in the mirror or I won't wake up again.

If you bruise your shin you shouldn't poke at the purple.
     There is a bruise in my head, it hurts either way.

Why do I feel such guilt for something I have not lost?
     And why do I feel such shame for never finding it?

They say I think therefore I am,
  I say I will only be once these thoughts are no longer mine.

They say to tell them, speak them, voice them and I'll be free.
     My tongue against my teeth says I do not have the key.

And the things that I have lost do not leave me, they clot under my skin.
                    A tapestry of swellings remind me of where I have been,
                                      and how far is left to go.
      I imagine death so much I feel as though it happened yesterday.
Did I kill him?

                                      I grind my back teeth.
Was it my fault?
                                        I puncture my lip.
I wasn't there.
                                      Why wasn't I there?
                                                Bite.

Everyone I ever know will someday die.
                                              Stop it. *Bite.*

These thoughts bleed like a gum without a tooth.
            I do not need to run my tongue over the gap to make it hurt.

I cannot tell you where it hurts
only that it does.

II

<u>Brushing teeth</u>

I begin the day by opening the curtains.
I press my forehead against the glass to see what is outside.
There is no traffic on the road.
                                      There is no traffic in my head.
In the mirror I see me grinning.
                                      I do not count my teeth.

BEYOND / TU HWNT

I pick apples from trees and bite them.
                My lips are not bruised, and my gums do not bleed.

The sun makes me laugh and I let myself smile.
The gravel paths grind under my boots.
                              My teeth are still.
My tea has two sugars,
                I drink wine from a hand-me-down glass.

I brush my teeth and think
            how much I would miss mundanity such as this
                      if I could never do it again.

1

BEYOND / TU HWNT

ADHD Thing

REBECCA WILSON

Sorry I don't live in that borough of London anymore.
I moved back to Wales for personal and financial reasons, so…

    I'm afraid you'll have to start the process again.

But I've already waited three years for my first assessment?

    Your information cannot be transferred across the border.

Dros y border yng Nghymru.

    Rhaid i chi aros tair blynedd am brawf ADHD, cariad.
    Sori, alla i wneud dim byd arall.

Mae'n iawn, dwi'n deall.
Dim bai ti 'di o.
Diolch am drio helpu.

    Sorry I can't be of more assistance.

It's ok, I understand.

ADHD THING / REBECCA WILSON

It's not your fault.
Thank you for trying to help.
Shit.

Shit. Shit. Shittedy. Shit balls. Shit faced. Shit fudge sprinkly. Shitty. Shit. Shit.

Another three years trying to navigate the overload
       the endlessly spinning plates
              while my mind shifts gears
from first
        to second
                to third
                        never pulling over

Intensity is the only key to calm.
Forcing my brain to focus.

Spontaneous bursts settle her.
When the dopamine hits, I can breathe.

        But it's not official.

I can't really say I have ADHD.

        You've been watching too much of that TikTok.

I don't even have TikTok.

I have
friends who have been diagnosed who tell me I
                        should get a test too.

I have
a self-assessment form from a GP that tells me I

                                              most likely have it.

And I have
a family who tell me

                                                it's just your personality.

You're fun, spontaneous, chatty, sunshine, creative, a bit crazy, weird, quirky, loud, annoying, keen, ask too many questions, a fidgeter, that girl who's always busy, who hates days off, who can't concentrate on one thing at a time, gets bored –

                                                      I get that too.

                                      Everyone feels that sometimes.

Sometimes.
Only sometimes.

                            When do you stop?
                    How do you have the energy?
                                    You're a lot, you know?
                    Too much.
                  Can't you sit and chill?
                              You don't have to say anything,
                          We could sit in silence.
                  Why can't you just relax?

I don't know, hun.

Because NHS England won't talk to NHS Wales.

So gad i fi fod.

So leave me alone.

Actually, can you stay? 'Cause I'll be bored in an ADHD 1, 2, 3...

Masked

FREYA F. ELLIOTT

Each long day I wear her pallid skin
I pull it on over my bones
and feel her smile stretch over my teeth
I hear her voice – my voice – speak
as I watch out of her glassy eyes like windows
afraid of being caught – of being seen
behind the mask – a complete fraud
frolicking in the body of an entirely *typical* girl
sometimes I'm not sure who I could be
without her.
I've worn her so long
her skin has fused with my bones
inseparable – until
I don't know which one of us is real.

If one day her skin should start to rot away
and peel back over my gums
would you finally be able to see me
as I truly am?

Clinig a Dwy Gacen

SIÂN ROBERTS

Yno ro'n i, yn agosáu at y ffin rhwng 'pum munud bach arall' a 'cachu hwch, dwi'n hwyr eto!' pan ganodd fy watsh. (Da 'di watsh sy hefyd yn ffôn. Mae'n anfon ambiwlans yn otomatig os ydw i'n syrthio a ddim yn symud – medden nhw!)

Gareth. 'Ti 'di codi?'

'Fwy neu lai.'

'Llai, felly. Gwranda, 'di'r llo 'ma byth 'di cyrraedd. Beryg fydd raid i mi gael ffariar. Fedri di gael rhywun arall i fynd efo chdi i'r clinig?'

'Fydda i'n iawn. 'Mond i weld nyrs dwi'n mynd.'

'Gofyn i un o'r plant.'

'Fydda i'n iawn.' Roedd yr antur o fynd ar fy mhen fy hun yn dechrau apelio.

'Neu Mari. Mae hi 'di ymddeol. Gewch chi fynd am fwyd wedyn.'

'Fydda i'n iawn ar 'y mhen 'yn hun. Dyna pam gawson ni'r car 'ma, cofio? Otomatig, drws bŵt rimôt contrôl a hoist.'

'Well i ti fynd â rhywun efo chdi.'

'Sawl gwaith sy isio deud? Dos!'

'Wel, paid â'n ffonio i os ti'n styc!'

'Dos!'

Jest y peth, ffrae cyn codi! Mae Gareth yn dda iawn, yn gwybod pryd i helpu a phryd i adael i mi roi cynnig arni – ac i fod wrth law pan dwi'n methu. Ond, weithiau, mae'n cymryd rôl y gofalwr ormod o ddifri. Dwi'n trio cofio bod ei fywyd yntau wedi newid pan ges i'r diagnosis. Weithiau, mae'n anodd derbyn 'mod i'n pwyso ar ei fraich yn lle gafael yn ei law. Ond tasen ni'n dal i gerdded law yn llaw yn ein hoed ni, fyddai pobl yn meddwl mai fisitors oedden ni!

Reit. Casglu'r nerth i godi, 'molchi a gwisgo. Ond mae meddwl am frecwast o goffi da, a bara efo mêl lleol yn hwb bob amser.

Cychwyn am yr ysbyty cyn i Gareth roi stop arna i.

Wrth i mi godi fy nghoes i'r car, tecst ar fy watsh.

'Cofia ffonio os bydd angen. Wnei di'n grêt. x'

'OK. Gwnaf siŵr! xx'

Ro'n i heb yrru ers wythnosau ond, cyn pen dim, ro'n i'n gyfforddus tu ôl i'r llyw. Bron nad o'n i'n teimlo'r gwynt yn fy ngwallt. Bach o fiwsig – *Moelyci*. Ro'n i'n gwenu fel giât wrth feddwl amdanaf fy hun fel un o'r 'mulod gwantan' ond 'Ymlaen mae Canaan'!

Cyrraedd yr ysbyty – lle hwylus i barcio. Un o fanteision prin bod yn anabl! Ar ôl byta banana – fy ateb i bob problem – ro'n i'n barod i ddadlwytho'r sgwter.

Difaru nad o'n i wedi mynnu gwneud yn amlach, ond roedd hi gymaint yn haws gadael i Gareth wneud.

Wrth i'r hoist ostwng y sgwter, sylwais fod gen i gwmni. Dyn mwstasiog, sigârog, â ffon braff.

'Jolly good,' meddai wrth i mi ddatod y llinynnau. Wir! 'I can set it up for you. I was an engineer.'

'It's fine, thanks. I'll manage,' medde fi'n biwis gan obeithio y diflannai cyn i mi wneud llanast ohoni. Mi safodd a gwylio – yn gwingo eisiau helpu. Ceisiais beidio ag edrych yn rhy smyg wrth gychwyn am y clinig.

Yn yr ystafell aros, gwelais ŵr a gwraig iau na mi yn 'studio'r sgwter. Gwenais. 'Hwn yn beth handi,' meddai'r gŵr, 'MS sy arnoch chithau hefyd?'

'Ie, ers rhai blynyddoedd. A chi?'

'Maria yn fama. Newydd gael gwybod. Dod i weld y Nyrs MS am y tro cynta.'

'Peidiwch â phoeni,' medde fi, gan geisio denu Maria i'r sgwrs, 'mae'n glên. Barod i wrando a'n 'neud ei gorau i helpu. Bosib welwch chi'r OT hefyd – mae hi'n gallu trefnu pethe handi o gwmpas y tŷ pan fydd angen – os bydd angen.'

'Mae cymaint i'w ddysgu, 'toes? Mae 'mhen i'n troi. Pawb yn deud pethe gwahanol,' mentrodd Maria.

'Hollol,' atebais. 'Mae pawb a'i nain yn meddwl eu bod nhw'n helpu trwy anfon lincs i wefannau doji sy'n addo gwnewch chi wella os prynwch chi eu stwff nhw neu sticio at ddeiet o frocoli a bîns, neu rywbeth.

'Mae'n well peidio gwglo – jest sticio at wefannau call. Mae'r Gymdeithas MS reit dda ac mae cwpwl o grwpiau Facebook da sy'n trafod petha ymarferol, fel pa sgidia sy'n dda. Y peth pwysica, am wn i, ydi peidio disgwyl gwyrthiau a derbyn bob help.'

'Ond maen nhw wrthi'n gweithio'n galed ar ffyrdd o'i wella,' mynnai'r gŵr.

'Ydyn, ond well gen i beidio â disgwyl gormod,' atebais braidd yn llipa gan obeithio nad o'n i wedi diffodd gobaith Maria.

Daeth y nyrs i 'ngalw i mewn, felly dyma roi fy enw Facebook i Maria a dweud wrthi am gysylltu os oedd hi ffansi.

Roedd y therapydd galwedigaethol yno hefyd ac mi gawson ni sgwrs ddigon buddiol. Trefnwyd i ni gael 'traed eliffant' o dan y gwely i'm helpu i godi a soniodd y nyrs am dabledi a allai helpu â'r cerdded. Dydyn nhw ddim yn gweithio i bawb ac mae'r sgileffeithiau'n gallu bod yn gas, ond ges i daflen i'w darllen. Gawn ni weld.

Wrth i mi adael, roedd Maria'n cael ei galw i mewn. Daeth lwmp i 'ngwddw wrth feddwl amdani'n dechrau ar ei thaith.

Reit, tŷ bach. Un peth da am doiledau ysbytai ydi bod y drysau'n agor y ddwy ffordd fel bod modd gyrru'r sgwter i mewn a bacio allan. Dau beth sydd ddim cystal yw bod y toiledau, yn aml, o uchder cyffredin, yn lle bod yn uwch, a bod pwy bynnag sy'n gosod y rêls codi fel pe bai'n chwarae 'sticio cynffon ar y mul' â mwgwd am ei lygaid, heb feddwl bod angen i rywun afael ynddyn nhw a rhoi ei bwysau arnyn nhw. Ond doedd gen i ddim amser i feddwl am fanion felly. Cyn gynted ag y mae fy ymennydd yn anfon neges i 'mhledren i ddweud bod gobaith ymwacáu, does dim eiliad i'w gwastraffu! Wff, jest mewn pryd. Ond wedyn, sut i godi o sêt isel heb allu cyrraedd y rêls? Rois i gynnig ar bwyso 'nwylo ar sêt y toilet – Ych! – a gwthio fy hun i fyny ond roedd y sêt yn rhy isel. Ro'n i'n styc. Ddylwn i dynnu'r llinyn coch rŵan a minnau'n dal yn weddol urddasol er 'mod i'n eistedd ar y tŷ bach, neu roi cynnig arall ar godi, â'r posibilrwydd o syrthio a cholli pob urddas? Allwn i gyrraedd y llinyn coch wedyn? Fyddai'r peth argyfwng ar fy watsh yn gweithio? Oedd digon o signal i ffonio? Am faint fyddwn i ar y llawr cyn cael fy ffeindio? Beth fyddai'n digwydd pe bawn i'n tynnu'r llinyn coch? Larwm dros bob man? Llais yn gofyn beth oedd yn bod? Fydden nhw'n gallu fy ngweld i trwy CCTV? Byddin o weithwyr yn cyrraedd i fy achub? Doeddwn i ddim cweit yn barod i fentro hynny er 'mod i'n chwys domen. A do'n i wir ddim isio rhoi cyfle i Gareth ddweud 'Udishido.'

Reit, meddwl clir. Tybed allwn i droi ar sgiw-wiff a chyrraedd handlbar y sgwter? Fyddai o'n ddigon cadarn i 'nal i? Dim ond un ffordd o ffeindio. Llaw chwith ar y sgwter, llaw dde jest abowt yn cyrraedd y reilen ar y wal, dwy droed yn solet ar y llawr, siglo 'nôl a 'mlaen dipyn, un ymdrech anferthol ond na, drato, dim cweit. Iste eto. Un cynnig arall. Taswn i'n methu fyddai gen i ddim nerth i dreio eto. Rhyddhad!

Er 'mod i'n ysu i adael y lle ar frys, pwyllais. Ro'n i'n benderfynol o gwyno – pa synnwyr mewn cael toilet ar gyfer pobl anabl os yw'n anaddas i bobl anabl? Dwi'n gwybod bod pob math o anableddau ond welais i erioed neb â breichiau pedair troedfedd! Mewn ysbyty, dydi pobl ag anableddau ddim yn brin. Dwi 'di gweld gwell toiledau mewn garejys, a hyd yn oed mewn lle amiwsments.

Ro'n i'n flin. Yn flin iawn. Ond ro'n i'n gwybod, unwaith y byddwn i'n gadael, y byddwn i'n gohirio anfon cwyn nes i'r peth ymddangos yn ddibwys, felly doedd dim amdani ond taro tra oedd yr haearn yn boeth.

Es at y ddesg, yn barod i sodro pwy bynnag oedd yn gyfrifol am y fath anfadwaith. Ond fel ro'n i'n agor fy ngheg, mi feddalais, a gofyn yn glên sut oedd mynd ati i gwyno. Byddai llythyr bach twt yn gwneud y tro yn iawn.

Pam roedd y dyn moel tu ôl i'r ddesg yn gwenu fel'na? O'n i'n ei nabod? O, na! Andriw Annoying o'r ysgol! Ro'n i'n gegagored.

'Andriw?'

'Delyth! Ti heb newid dim!'

'Go brin!'

Ar ôl sgwrs sydyn, 'Sut wyt ti?', 'Sut wyt tithau?', ro'n i'n barod i fynd ond gofynnodd, 'Ti'n barod am ginio? Dretia i ti yn y cantîn. Dwi'n cael disgownt staff.'

'Dyna gynnig na fedra i mo'i wrthod!'

Yn y cantîn, mi ffeindiodd Andriw fwrdd a symud cadair i wneud lle i'r sgwter yn ddiffwdan. Tra oedd o'n nôl y bwyd, tecstiais i Gareth yn sydyn, 'Popeth wedi mynd yn iawn. Cinio yn y cantîn efo hen ffrind ysgol. x'

Dros bei pysgod a *chips* main, a phaned, gawson ni sgwrs ddigon hwyliog am ddyddiau ysgol a hanes hwn a'r llall. Yna,

'Reit, deuda'n iawn, sut wyt ti? Neu ydi hynna'n beth powld i ofyn a titha'n gorfod iwsio hwnna?' nodiodd at y sgwter.

'Wel, doedd MS ddim yn rhan o'r plan, ond mi allai fod lot gwaeth. Dwi'm yn meddwl amdano fel "gorfod", neu bod yn "gaeth i gadair olwyn". Mae'n rhoi rhyddid i fi fynd i lefydd ar 'y mhen 'yn hunan. Fel hyn!'

'Un gall fuost ti erioed!'

Nid dyna oedd ei farn pan rois i lond ceg iddo am pingio 'mra i pan oedd o'n iste tu ôl i fi yn Geog, Fform Tŵ, ond wnes i ddim o'i atgoffa.

'Sut mae'r MS 'ma'n effeithio arnat ti 'te?'

'O, timbo, 'Pen, ysgwyddau, coesau, traed, coesau, traed,

pen, ysgwyddau, coesau, traed, coesau, traed,

llygaid, clustiau, trwyn a cheg,

pen, ysgwyddau, coesau, traed, coesau, traed' (efo'r mosiwns) a dipyn bach o bobman yn y canol hefyd.'

Roedd y ddau ohonon ni'n giglan fel tasen ni 'nôl yn 'rysgol.

'Wel, dio ddim 'di effeithio ar dy hiwmor di, beth bynnag.'

'Nacdi, diolch byth, neu fyse hi wedi canu arna i. Reit, dwi'n mynd – neu fydda i angen mynd i'r tŷ bach eto.'

'Paid â phoeni, ga i oriad os bydd angen.'

'Dwi'n mynd. Rŵan.'

'Tisio help i gal hwnna 'nôl yn car?' Wnes i ddim gwrthod tro 'ma.

I ffwrdd â fi a Steve Eaves yn gwmni eto.

Er 'mod i wedi cael mwy na digon o antur am un diwrnod, do'n i ddim cweit yn barod i fynd adre.

Penderfynais aros yn y ganolfan-arddio-a-thipyn-o-bopeth i gael fy meddwl at ei gilydd. Ar ôl pip yn yr adrannau dillad a bwyd drud-ond-neis, es i am y caffi. Aeth un o'r merched â 'mhaned a 'nghacen at y bwrdd a symud cadair heb i mi ofyn, chwarae teg.

Reit, penderfyniad. Oeddwn i am ddweud wrth Gareth am drafferth y tŷ bach?

Penderfynu peidio. Fyddai o'n flin efo'r ysbyty ac yn fwy cyndyn o 'ngadael i allan ar fy mhen fy hun!

Tŷ bach cyn cychwyn adre? Falle ddim.

Ymlaen mae Canaan.

Adre. Gareth wedi rhoi dillad ar lein. Arwydd da. Car Gethin ar yr iard. A cyn i fi dynnu fy nghoes wan o'r car...

'Ydi'r nyrs wedi 'neud dy goes di'n well, Nain?'

'Nadi, cofia, Deio, ddim yn well, ond dwi am gael pethe o'r enw traed eliffant i roi dan y gwely i'n helpu i i godi.'

'Eliffant go iawn?'

'Eliffant smalio.'

'Biti.'

A dyma hithau, Mari.

''Dan ni wedi 'neud cacen i ti a Taid. Ac wedi'i haddurno hi.

Ond mae Deio wedi rhoi'i fys yn yr eisin.'

'Dim ond bys bach oedd o.'

'Dwi'n siŵr bydd hi'n hyfryd. Cerwch i ddeud wrth Taid am roi'r tegell ymlaen.'

Ac i ffwrdd â nhw gan roi munud i fi dynnu 'nghoes wan o'r car, estyn fy ffyn a gwneud fy ffordd gan bwyll i'r tŷ.

Gwên fawr. 'Be 'di hanes y fuwch?'

'Y llo'n sugno rêl boi. Sut aeth hi efo chdi? Pwy 'di'r hen ffrind 'ma?'

'Andriw Annoying oedden ni'n ei alw fo yn 'rysgol. Mae o i weld yn reit normal erbyn hyn. Reit, lle mae'r gacen 'ma? Dwi jest yn picio i'r tŷ bach.'

Recognition

SAM SKELTON

I

In 2019, I take a trip abroad for a holiday.
On the way back, at Gatwick Airport, I stand in one of the long lines at passport control. My family in front of me pass through.
When I get to the scanner, I stand on the designated markings and wait for the gates to open. A red light flashes. The passengers behind me bristle. I try again. Red, again.
I call to a woman sitting on a grown-up high chair in a blue and red airline suit.
'Excuse me. I don't think it's working.'
'Try again.'
'I already did.'
Everyone in the line can hear me.
'I've had an operation on my face since the photo was taken.'
She replies: 'You shouldn't have chosen it then.'

I shouldn't have chosen it. What choice did I have?
I had cancer on my face.
It's not a choice to have part of your face scraped off.
You think I wanted this?

She means the passport control line with facial recognition.
'No, I'm sorry. I didn't realise.'
She sucks her teeth.
'Please can you help me out of here.'
With reluctance she ushers the queue to the side.
I back out face down, saying sorry repeatedly to tutting passengers.
I am apologising for my face.

II

In 2021 I buy a new mobile phone with facial recognition software. To set it up it scans your face several times. Thereafter whenever you want to 'open' your phone it gazes at you and allows access. This phone has only seen me with my scars. It has registered them as my authorised image.

On the days when my face no longer feels like my own, I open my phone repeatedly to check if I am me.

Face

SAM SKELTON

I am sitting in front of my mirror. Not just any mirror but one carefully chosen; deliberately aged, slightly distressed, with a sepia hue that banishes stark outlines.

My image, in particles of light, streams towards the glass then bounces off the smooth surface. Everything in front of the mirror is reflected backwards, retracing the path it travelled to get there. This is how mirrors really work. My reflection is not reversed or switched left to right, up or down. It is inverted front to back. I am coming and going at the same time. My face was. My face is. My face was. Is again.

I observe this visage, deliberately obfuscated, arriving and departing in my antiqued mirror. It is a trick: I am not seen, then unseen. My face is constant in its adoption of my selfness. My old image was so familiar.

This new one, stitched to me with needle and thread, feels like an unrelenting stranger. This face is a narcissist so concerned with who sees it, how it is interpreted, what it represents. It imprints itself on my unwilling mind's eye, cracking its way through the glass when all I want is my old image back.

Perhaps I am too unkind. What was and what is, the past and the present, seeks unity, consolation, acceptance. I try to meet my new face without judgement, but I am girding my body and whispering reassurances to the rest of me that not everything has changed.

BEYOND / TU HWNT

The Red and White Inhaler

GUINEVERE CLARK

Kissed wide and daily spit, shared
shifter of morning's notch,
the addiction or need –
that dilator, inhaler, the calm
and stop with coffee, I suck
into the secret of my
tattered bronchus. Vital
friend, waker of powder-burst,
scuffed in the bag, stockpiled,
cooled, can never lose you,
lips reaching, I'm huffed up,
to cough, whisper in your pale
funnel – softly dusted with us.

1

Criminal Bodies

MATTHEW HAIGH
after David Cronenberg's 'Crimes of the Future'

1

In this bed whose bulk is a gastropod
flipped on its back, I attempt to reconfigure

the pinch points of myself, to work the lathe
of spinal column, rise and ambulate.

A world well-designed for you, ill-equipped for me, awaits.
You perch bird-light on the counter, bacon flapping

on your fork, as if you have evolved
beyond infection risk or hurt.

I move through the day doing admin, wearing
my veins like a threadbare carpet.

How to make art from anarchy – take my body's
concertinaed bone key, call it to order?

2

Language fails.
Is a volley of birds
splatting on glass.

You know it when she asks
how are you or they ask feeling better now?
Filling forms

in which letters are brittle castles spilling out the stale kings.
Wild to think words accommodate
or a single body could contain
a cosmic-level horror.

3

Organ failure, a dodgy hip or crap scapula –
endless ways to go 'wrong'

to be seen to be committing a biological crime.
Absorbing the microplastics
that bleed from a poisonous industry

I tiptoe past
a strict government's searchlight eye,
who set a financial threshold on our pain, who register
and classify

our bodies, modify the data.

4

A pantheon of pipe work, the unemployed self
a dilapidated factory void and haunted

by productivity's cache.
Easy to feel small

in bugger-all towns,
knowing days that emulsify

into the strangest lotion. I saw a painting of
a church webbed in living tissue, thought *same*.

Crouched here, undiscovered. Little cryptid.

Grateful

DEE MONTAGUE

I live in a body that doesn't follow rules.
She often rebels, cuts ties to gratitude;
my world becomes dark, shrunken to one room,
I'm prescribed rest, positivity, and platitudes.

But for the small things I am grateful;
mugs of hot tea presented with love,
comfort telly and snacks by the plateful.
When my world grows, the sun caresses my face
and the breeze whispers its secrets in my hair.

Because of – not despite – being disabled,
I am changed. I have grown. Empathy overflows.
I am gracious with love – and black humour.
I am joyful, compassionate, tenacious.
I am grateful.

/

Untethered

PAUL DAVIES

An avalanche of rain drops sting my cheeks. The autumn air chills my bones. As I breathe in the grayscale scene, I know I'm home.

The promised storm has only just set in, but the mountain fog has already shrouded the views that make Bannau Brycheiniog the spiritual home of sunset snaps and hashtag hiking. If some other soggy soul has joined me on my pilgrimage, I can't see them.

I exist alone in this waterlogged world of jagged rocks and naked mud. The wind runs wild, breathing life into the stubborn shrubs who cling to the hillside in defiance. Every inch is a warning to go cautiously, but one I read as an invitation to let go.

Against the day's monochrome palette, I am a flash flood of colour. My leopard print leggings and clashing pink t-shirt are a rebellion against the voice – implanted in my head – telling me not to stand out.

I hurtle down uneven tracks with my feet moving to the rhythm of my pounding heart. As I run, mind, body and soul slip into sync.

While I wonder what's ahead, my feet find out. By the time my brain grows tired of my surroundings, I've already left them behind. My mind is finally untethered and my body matches its relentless pace.

All that matters is what I feel in that moment; the wind jostling my jacket, the rain water rolling down my back, the earth ever-changing under my searching feet.

There is freedom in the frantic as I escape the chains of conformity that bind me – a square peg man in a world of round-shaped holes. I have, however briefly, escaped an existence where I am pursued by promises of productivity and haunted by an absence of purpose.

I outrun the labels that chase me and each stride sees me redefine myself within this rugged reality. They say I'm inattentive but here I am consumed. They say I'm restless but here I find calm in chaos. They say I'm impulsive but here it becomes the very thing that keeps me on my feet.

I barely remember the world of anxiety and depression, where people are more concerned with who I should be than who I am meant to be. The mountain reveals my purest form.

On the trails – without a destination, a plan, nor reason – I become a physical manifestation of my internal restlessness. A juxtaposition of joy and jeopardy.

Feeling

                    N
        E   D
                L

                            E

                                  S
                                    S

in moments that can't last forever.

Night Storms

LEIGH MANLEY

The thudding thrombus / eventide burrows /
stirs my curdled blood / precipitates the tapping
tempest / wasteland's sleeping flood / the shrouded
bundle weathers / severs plagues of night / spears rain
translations / disturbing raven's flight / the tipping
squall abandons / free-falling shadows spill / awaken
in the eiderdown / spitting morning's pill.

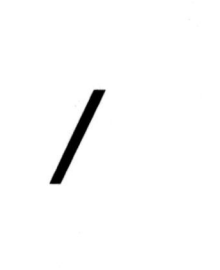

ously # Dyslexia, Dyspraxia & Desperation: The World of Work

DIFFWYS CRIAFOL

> *'Just knowing your rights (or your worth or value) will never be enough if you are powerless to force someone else to respect them.'*
>
> **Alice Wong**
> *Disability Visibility: First-Person Stories from the Twenty-first Century*

I was diagnosed in a haphazard way with dyslexia and dyspraxia while at university. I had requested to write my philosophy essays through the medium of Welsh – because, under the Welsh Language Act of 1993, it was my right. However, the department inferred from this that I just wasn't 'confident' in working in English as a native Welsh speaker. I was then referred to the University's English Language Centre, a service usually for international students to gain support with their English language skills. This was supposed to give me extra support so that I could eventually transition to writing my philosophy essays in English.

I went but grudgingly – they already had me down as a troublemaker. I had a legal right to study in my mother tongue and believed it to be a matter of principle. Hundreds of people had gone to prison for our language rights in the twentieth century. However this was before the days of the Coleg Cymraeg Cenedlaethol: studying in the medium of Welsh at university wasn't taken seriously for the most part. It was seen as an inconvenience.

I remember writing a few sentences down, doing the exercises with the tutor. After only a few minutes he stopped me and said that he thought I almost certainly had dyslexia. Where I'd spelt words incorrectly, the letters were 'jumbled up'. It seemed completely obvious to him. I was then sent packing for the drawn-out process of getting an assessment.

Around six months later, after several tests and a session of several hours with an educational psychologist, I was diagnosed not only with dyslexia but a thing I had never heard of before, dyspraxia – a condition that meant a lack of physical coordination at its core that also impacted the way I managed structure and order when writing.

This explained a lot – I was somewhat relieved. I had been put in the low 'sets' at school in English specifically due to my issues with spelling. I felt let down – dyslexia seemed to have affected my English in a far greater way than my Welsh, which is a much more phonetic language.

The educational psychologist said I was a 'compensative dyslexic'. Perhaps the strategies I used to mask my dyslexia were more effective in Welsh. I was an avid reader and always felt jealous of my friends being allowed to analyse more challenging texts while we watched the *Romeo and Juliet* film on repeat in our lower-tier English class. I felt hopeful that this diagnosis would be a game changer, and the obstacles these specific learning difficulties presented could be remedied by the system. I was wrong.

When I resolved to do my course through the medium of Welsh, the university struggled to provide me with support on a par with those who were receiving support in English. I had several different dyslexia support staff working with me. Some tried to retro-fit techniques for dyslexia in English to Welsh that just didn't work. One tutor couldn't write in Welsh and only had basic spoken Welsh language skills. By this point I had changed subjects, burnt out from the lack of support to study philosophy in my chosen language. I was now studying a degree in Welsh.

They told me that I was the first person to request dyslexia support through the medium of Welsh so it just didn't exist. I felt sceptical. No one had any idea how to support me with the issues that came up with dyspraxia short of recommending I buy colourful stationery and an organiser. I did receive a laptop which I was very grateful for – there was some transcription software on it but there was no training on how to use it, and of course when I experimented with it, it didn't understand my accent and only operated in English.

My hopes for a more equal playing field were eroded, and I stopped engaging with the support services at the university.

Fast forward to the world of work; things went from bad to worse.

I remember having an informal meeting with a colleague – we were organising an intense, fast-paced event. It was the middle of a week-long Welsh language festival. I had been sleeping, eating and breathing the work and was running on adrenaline. My colleague and I were friends and having gone to Cambridge, he was highly educated. As we were chatting and I was jotting down my own action points, he said, 'Sorry, I just have to do this...' He then proceeded to take my notebook and pen out of my hand, and went on to correct the spelling of the notes I had been writing in front of me.

As he handed me back my notebook my eyes stung hot as I attempted to bite back the tears. Humiliation and anger felt acutely physical at that moment, but I didn't want to make him feel uncomfortable. I just continued as if nothing had happened, hoping he hadn't noticed the blood rushing to my face and the film of tears over my eyes – I didn't dare blink for fear of them streaming down my cheeks. It was a culmination of a lifetime of people making assumptions about my intelligence based on how I write.

As a woman in my early twenties from a working class background with a strong regional accent, I was used to being patronised, but this small gesture was different. I never spoke to him about how it made me feel, and maybe I should have. The fact that he had been to Cambridge, and was very middle class added to the awkward power dynamic which made this interaction feel particularly jarring.

The friend had made an innocent mistake, not knowing how much this small action would affect me. He told me previously that he had been brought up by parents who, as a child, didn't let him play with children who lived in council houses. It was clear he had more to unlearn in terms of classism than most. I don't hold any bad feelings towards him.

**

Other experiences I have are a little less easy for me to make sense of. I started working in the third sector at a job I loved and felt I was doing well in – an event I was organising had even won a national award. One morning I was writing a press release for a 'Papur Bro'. These are local Welsh-language papers run by volunteers in a local community focusing on local matters.

**

When I wrote the press release, I used a warm, informal tone as was usual for these types of community publications. My boss was old-fashioned and didn't like working digitally, so as instructed I printed the press release and took it to her to have a look at before I sent it out as it was about a major festival we were planning.

Like a teacher, she proceeded with her red pen to underline and circle my jumbled letters or words she didn't like. When she reached halfway down the page she scribbled a cross across the whole page and tossed the piece of paper back at me. This made me feel like a child and it repulsed me. The physical sensations of humiliation gripped my body, from my stomach to my throat; it was a visceral reaction.

She reprimanded me for how I had written the press release, that it shouldn't be so informal. Despite having used the Welsh language spell check, it hadn't caught everything (it never does) and she reprimanded my spelling too.

I told her with tears streaming down my face that I had made them aware already that I had been diagnosed with dyslexia and dyspraxia, that as an employer she was obligated legally to make reasonable adjustments for this, that I had asked for this several times.

She responded by scoffing at me saying this was nonsense.

The class dynamic came into this again – the intersection of class, intellectual snobbery and disability converge in a way that makes it especially difficult to weather this kind of treatment. This incident was the last straw in several of being at the mercy of my boss's mood swings. Some days she would be great to work with, days like this out of nowhere I felt like a punchbag. I shortly found another (less well paid) job, and I left.

The curse of my dyslexia, or rather people's disabling attitude towards it didn't end there. In one of my first jobs in journalism, a field that I was overjoyed to be working in, I ran into the same old attitudes. Most of my colleagues were friendly and welcoming, however, one person suddenly got very upset with me for sending her some questions in the form of voice notes.

I feel embarrassed by my spelling, and I can't install spell check on my devices because I work multilingually. When I send a written text message I always have some anxiety about sounding like I'm so stupid that I can't write. Checking my spelling before each text, the process of copy and pasting the writing into another piece of spell check software is labour-intensive, therefore voice notes have been a good solution for me.

This colleague got angry with me for 'wasting her time' by sending voice notes. She then proceeded to complain about me sending voice notes rather than texts to our line manager and other colleagues. She knew I was dyslexic and I was perplexed by her behaviour. My line manager was understanding. The colleague who had complained about me was privately educated; it all just felt like an old pattern repeating itself.

My relationship with this colleague deteriorated and again my working environment eventually became unbearable. She began to look at my work without me knowing on our shared cloud drive and then complaining to my line manager about faults in my unfinished work. She also scuppered a month of research on a company we were commissioned to write about because her friend worked there, and told her at a party that 'they were ethical' and there was no need for us to publish anything about them. My line manager was abroad so there was nothing that could be done about it.

* * *

Another junior colleague, who had a diagnosis of ADHD, had also been treated badly and felt it was fuelled by ableism. She told me that in a research training session, they had used an example of a real mistake I had made during my training period as an example of 'what not to do'. She proceeded to joke about 'this is what you know who did' in front of everyone as they delivered the training. Three of us left the cooperative of five people due to the way we were being treated.

Instead of being able to celebrate or even accept my neurodiversity, I felt cursed by it. This had happened too many times for me to bear and my self-esteem was in tatters. I felt like a waste of space and unable to imagine a future where I could thrive. My dyspraxia made me feel that I was ill-suited for any practical work that required a level of coordination. I had considered studying to be a nurse but because of how bad my co-ordination was I thought it wouldn't be a good idea. A friend of mine joked that she would be scared if she got me as a nurse with how clumsy I was. I also felt relegated from the world of thought, since being dyslexic meant that my written work would always be poor. I felt anxious about trying to find another job and landing myself in another difficult situation.

I started to write freelance, looking for opportunities to express myself. With a hunger to share my experiences, mostly those centred around class – it just sort of happened.

* * *

Today my relationship with my dyslexia has thawed. This has in large part been the result of small successes with my writing during the past year. I won a writing competition and got a place on an author development programme. Having to spend triple the time checking my own work for errors and dealing with structural issues that stem from dyspraxia in writing is an inconvenience but it's not the end of the world.

I've taken to writing in English – the inverse of my experience at school is now the case. Because spell check in the Welsh language is comparatively underdeveloped and more difficult to access, it's now more challenging for me to write articles in Welsh without needing a level of support that I don't have when it comes to proofreading. Dyslexia, or rather the lack of the accessibility software I need has estranged me from writing in my mother tongue. However, with the support of a small independent publisher I'm in the process of editing my first essays that will be published in Welsh.

Over the years I have been diagnosed with a plethora of conditions. From Obsessive Compulsive Disorder to Generalised Anxiety Disorder, from Developmental Trauma to more recently a councillor telling me that I need an assessment for ADHD. The overlap between dyslexia, dyspraxia and all these conditions, not to mention the fact that these things inevitably intersect and interact with things such as my gender and class make it hard to untangle what condition causes what in my life. Although labels have their uses, I've felt alienated by the pathologization of my personality.

My longest time in any employment was two years. My average is six months. I've never been sacked, but I leave workplaces when I see that things aren't working. I can dream of writing for a living although I know this isn't realistic for me. I'm still working out what to do with my life while parenting a young child.

The system denies me access to the tools and support I need, however the very same system demands that I produce work that is palatable to an imaginary audience who fit an ableist 'norm'.

* * *

In analysing my experience the social model of disability illustrates the situation well. This is a concept emergent from the disability rights movement between the 1970s and 1980s. It conveys that the barriers we face are the result of not being accommodated by society. It is not our differences themselves that disable us; the social model of disability conveys that the barriers we face are the result of not being accommodated by society.

As my experience with Welsh, English and writing reveals – my specific learning difficulty could be addressed if the will to do so was there. In a capitalist society, despite the efforts to superficially support people with 'protected characteristics', disabled people can feel like burdens in the workplace.

Dyslexia and dyspraxia have meant I have always had a complex relationship with words. As I write, I attempt to process experiences of family and friends in prison, the death of friends, of precarious housing, being a mother and within capitalist modernity, whilst also taking stock of my positionality as a white, disabled, working class cis woman, with an array of other things complicating my life. The irony of using writing in order to better understand myself and the world is not lost on me.

Burning Shame

RACHEL CARNEY

I hurl the words that haunt me
into a pit:

        'slow'   *'stubborn'*

            'lazy'   *'clumsy'*

              'rude'

I light a match and fling it in,
set fire to the words,
watch them curl and burn.

        'stupid'   *'weak'*

The heat intensifies.

BURNING SHAME / RACHEL CARNEY

I chuck in   *'must try harder'*

and breathe out,
slowly,
as it crackles
into ash.

Over time,
the mind
reclaims itself.

Smoke rises,
in mute wisps
of grey
and fragile black

Dysgu Dargyfeiriol

LEE GREEN

Ac onid ni
sy'n symudliwiau
yn y golau?
Cipolwg ar dragwyddoldeb
mewn llygad gwlyb madfall,
rhwbio ffyn
drosodd a
throsodd a
throsodd,
creu tân
i fynd â ni ymlaen.
Trown y crochan.
Rydym wedi chwilota'n llafurus,
pob gronyn wedi'i brosesu'n dyner,
pob ffibr
wedi ei smwddio
drosodd a
throsodd a
throsodd.
Yr heddwch a ddaw yn sgil hyn
yw gwerth ein diwydrwydd mwyn,

DYSGU DARGYFEIRIOL / LEE GREEN

ein gallu i ofalu,
i sylwi.
Nid yw ein meddyliau yn gweithio fel y llu:
rydym yn arloeswyr
lle mae eraill yn dilyn.
Rydym yn addasu,
ailadrodd a mireinio,
ailadrodd a mireinio
pob tasg, hyd heddiw –
ei hystyried yn ddwys:
y farddoniaeth a ddygwn,
ein holl newyddbethau.
Ailadrodd a mireinio
drosodd a throsodd
nes i donnau tawelwch
allyrru o ddawns ein bysedd.
Nid yw gair llafar yn dduw
ac mae ystyr i bethau eraill
heblaw llygad i llygad.

Dream*

SOFIA BRIZIO

'Dreams are some crazy, feminine, irrational, mad shit. Not serious, right? But we, disabled people, we dream a lot. In psych wards, of dead friends, of getting out of our parents' basement apartment, on day 645 of pandemic not-leaving-the-house, of lovers who will be sweet to us in autistic, Deaf, disabled ways... We go to bed every night dreaming of the disability justice future. And we will keep dreaming these wild disability justice dreams, every night and day, until we meet her.'

Leah LakshmI Piepzna-Samarasinha
The Future is Disabled

The first time I had that dream, I remember waking up on the floor, in a pool of my own sweat. I must have been about nine years old – definitely no older than ten, because at ten I'd stopped keeping the dream journal where I remember noting down the dream I'd had that morning.

It wasn't really a journal, rather a bunch of pages my grandpa let me rip from one of his old diaries that I had then stapled together. I had started noting down my dreams because that was what my psychiatrist told me to do, thinking it would make it easier for me to understand why I was afraid of the dark, balloons popping, fireworks and thunderstorms. I knew perfectly well that the reason for my fear of the dark was the absence of light, and the reason for my fear of things that popped was that, well, they *popped*. I couldn't see why I was supposed to enjoy having my eardrums shattered and why it was a problem that I didn't enjoy it. That made perfect sense to me and I had no issue writing down my nightmares filled with loud guns, giant balloons popping, and ghosts emerging from the darkness, because surely the only conclusion one could draw was that I was a sensitive child, and that was it.

This dream, though, was different. I was eager to write it down before I forgot all about it, but I wasn't so sure I would want to tell my psychiatrist about it. It seemed to me that everyone wanted my disability to be the culprit of whatever I was going through at any given time. 'It must be so difficult,' said my non-disabled psychiatrist, my non-disabled teacher, my non-disabled neighbour, as if they knew first-hand how it felt. In fact, they had no idea how non-difficult my life was. I had never known anything other than the wonky body I was born in, and I didn't want to change that. Everything felt easy because I had no idea that things could be and were supposed to be easier.

The dream caught me by surprise because I'd never dreamt of myself as disabled before, or rather, my disability never played a part in my dreams. It was just me, no mobility aids. Not because I didn't want them to be there, but because they just weren't relevant. A dream about my disability would be a goldmine for my psychiatrist, the holy grail of psychological issues, the perfect opportunity to utter the words she'd been holding back all along: 'The problem is your disability.' It mattered little that, on a regular day, my biggest problem was probably that the boy I liked from my class didn't say hi to me, or that I didn't want to finish the Harry Potter books because I had no idea what to read next. Not once did it occur to me that any of this might signal unresolved issues with my disability. I've always found it interesting that since this particular dream, I never dreamt of myself without my mobility aids again, at least not from what I can remember.

The dream felt like being in a watercolour painting whose delicate pastel tones I remember vividly nearly twenty years later. It felt like I was watching a film while simultaneously being able to control what I was doing. In the opening scene, I was sitting in my grandma's living room, on the teal sofa, surrounded by dusty books on a wooden shelf, and oil paintings hanging from the white walls. My walker was in front of me, just like it always was in real life.

I had a pill in the palm of my hand. It was pink and glittery – the two things I hated the most. I looked at it and then put it in my mouth without even questioning what it was, like it was something I did every day. It disappeared on my tongue. It didn't dissolve, I didn't taste the glitter nor the pink. It vanished as if it had never been there in the first place.

I was wearing a green watch on my right wrist, counting down from twelve hours.

11:59:59
11:59:58
11:59:57

I sat there, unsure what to do as I felt my body become lighter, the pain and fatigue subsiding. Then I stood up in one effortless movement, and walked out of the room, leaving my walker behind as if I had done it before.

A few moments later, I was in a dance studio. I started pacing up and down the wooden floor, admiring my body in the gigantic mirror. I couldn't believe I was standing on my own. It felt like the most natural thing in the world. It didn't even occur to me that gravity could trip me up at any moment. Balance was a mere afterthought in this new body of mine.

DREAM* / SOFIA BRIZIO

I threw one leg up in the air just to test it. I brought it back down and repeated the movement with the other leg. It worked: both legs functioned equally and they were the same length. I looked at my perfectly straight feet and touched the floor with both heels. I had never been able to do it in my usual body. The feeling of my feet spreading flat on the cold, smooth wooden floor made me dizzy with excitement. I tried to move one arm and one leg simultaneously and realised that, although it required little effort, I didn't really know how to do it properly. It was another one of those things I had never done in my usual body. I don't remember trying to dance. I never liked dancing much. I just kept walking, jumping, twirling occasionally, marvelling at my newfound agility. But I had no desire to dance nor run. It felt unnatural without my walker.

The imaginary camera in my dream suddenly cut to a new scene. An autumnal garden – my parents' garden. Every time I woke up from the dream, I remember thinking it looked exactly like the drawings in *Winnie the Pooh* and I loved it. In the garden, I walked on the carpet of red and brown leaves without having to worry about where my feet landed, looking up at the oak trees instead of down at my wheels. I climbed up one of the trees to admire the pink clouds playing in the sunset.

I had no idea how much time had passed between walking in the dance studio and climbing that tree in the garden, or how long I had been sitting on that branch looking at the orange sky and listening to the birds sing. When I glanced at my green watch, I only had one hour left.

The first time I had the dream, the morning I wrote it down, I thought that it was silly that I couldn't control time. It was *my dream*, after all. If I could control everything in it, why not time?

I found it ironic how quickly a dream could turn into a nightmare. Not a scary nightmare, though. The kind of nightmare that makes your skin crawl but that you wouldn't mind going back to every now and then, just to see how it ends, if it ever ends.

I started to feel uneasy, looking at the seconds flashing by on my watch.

00:59:59
00:59:58
00:59:57

I jumped off the tree and turned around, walking back towards my parents' house. I climbed a small hill leading to the main garden outside the front door, and there I saw my grandpa waiting for me, smiling. The sunlight glimmered in his green eyes, his white shirt and maroon trousers spotless against the autumnal backdrop. I hugged him and we danced to no music, but dancing like that, without worrying about my body, felt once again strange and unfamiliar.

I held my grandpa's hand and opted to walk instead, back towards the hill, to the brown bench where we'd always sit together and sing.

I expected him to start singing but instead he said, 'I don't like you like this. You're not *you*.'

I remained in silence. I know what he meant now, I thought about it enough in my waking hours, but at the time it was one of those dreamlike moments where you knew you'd say something back if it were a real conversation, but you don't because it's a dream and it doesn't have to make sense. The whole premise of the conversation didn't make sense.

So we started singing like we'd always do. I don't remember the song, but I know it must have been in Italian, as that was the only language we spoke. When the song ended, I glanced at my watch again and saw that I only had two minutes left. My heart started racing and tears welled up in my eyes. There were so many things I still wanted to do. I wanted to get dressed without feeling exhausted afterwards. I wanted to stand in the shower and use both my hands to wash my body and my hair. I wanted to go on a spontaneous trip without the endless planning and worrying. I still didn't want to run, though. I will never understand why people assume that the first thing I would want to do with a pair of functioning legs is run. I can't imagine it being a pleasant experience. I told myself that there would be other pills (ugly, pink, glittery pills), that I could have a non-disabled body again, whenever I wanted. But did I really want it?

As if he read my mind, Grandpa spoke again, 'If you take too many of those, you'll never be able to get back to your body, you know?'

I felt sick. I stood and started pacing back and forth by the bench. I wanted my body back. Was it wrong that I did, when that pill had given me everything I was supposed to want?

00:00:03
00:00:02
00:00:01
00:00:00

I felt something drag me down and I fell on my knees with a thud.

Except I wasn't on my knees. I was laying down on my bedroom floor, in a pool of my own sweat.

I smiled, thinking I was finally home.

I looked at my walker, felt my wonky body, painfully awake. I felt a surge of gratitude when I tried to get up and realised I couldn't.

Home.

*This is a fictional piece and the characters are not based on real people.

BEYOND / TU HWNT

Borderline Questionnaire

ZOË BRIGLEY

People with BPD face struggles of the condition on a daily basis, and often experience stigma, discrimination, isolation, and insults. Most of what's written about BPD doesn't sound overly positive with many being portrayed as manipulative, hopeless and dangerous. In fact, individuals presenting with BPD experience an extraordinarily rich and intense life of both highs and lows.

Borderline in the ACT
A charity at the Women's Centre for Health Matters

When feelings come, do they come as a storm?
Do you feel the pain of others like you feel your own?
Can you detect facial expressions?
Do you sense subtle mood swings?
Do you perceive fluctuations as disapproval?
Do you seem grounded and level to others?
Does love envelop you?
Have you ever escalated conflict?
Do you have intrusive thoughts?
Do you fear rejection?

BORDERLINE QUESTIONNAIRE / ZOË BRIGLEY

Do you fear disappointment?
Do you fear the label that you have been given?
How far would you go to avoid abandonment?
Are you candid and honest with others?
Do you depend on others?
Do you connect well with others?
Are you sensitive to beauty?
Do you have suicidal thoughts?
Have you built a life regardless?
Do you suffer pain privately?
Does your work encourage you?
Do you find comfort in a cause?
Do you idealise others?
Do you spend time daydreaming?
Do you lose yourself in the ecstatic?
Does believing in a god make you feel nurtured?
Are you fond of animals?
Would you describe yourself as impulsive?
Do you experience both positive and negative emotional states?
Have you learnt that feelings are like the weather?
Have you learnt that feelings pass like rain?

Baby-Led Healing

KATIE BENNETT-DAVIES

My alarm is going off again. Is it day or night? We're still in hospital after my C-section. We have a private double room so that my husband, Paul, can stay with me. I wouldn't be able to manage on my own as a Disabled person; we need to work as a team. Dopey-eyed, I switch on the light, which wakes Paul but our baby, Mabli, is still fast asleep. We begin the process of trying to wake her up. She's a sleepy baby so she doesn't give hunger cues until she's ravenous, making breastfeeding tougher. Despite feeding on demand being in vogue, we're sticking to a four-hour routine. Dispirited attempts at breastfeeding ended in Paul giving Mabli formula because she wasn't able to drink enough from me. She's already tiny, we can't afford for her not to be feeding well. I have hazy memories of midwives confirming that her latch is good, as is my supply. A seemingly endless parade of uniformed people come in and out of our room day and night. They all play the same tune – *you can do it*. However, trying to do the gymnastics needed to manipulate both Mabli's limbs and mine in order to feed properly is proving impossible. No one wants to suggest formula, least of all me. My fears about my inability to be a competent mum are no longer just nasty voices in my head, they are now in black and white on a child services report.

After a nappy change, lots of encouragement and some cold water, Mabli's eyes have the glazed look of an awake newborn. I try once more to put her to my breast. She latches and starts drinking. I smile with relief. I've done it. All this pain and exhaustion has been worth it. I'm finally a proper mum.

'Oh, baby's fallen asleep again,' the midwife says. I'd beeped her to come in and help with another feed, desperate to get the feeding right so we can all go home.

'This is exactly what keeps happening. I can't keep her awake and drinking long enough...' I complain. My eyes plead with her to tell me what I'm doing wrong.

The midwife looks at me empathetically. She sits on the bed. 'Do you really want to breastfeed? It's perfectly ok if you want to formula feed. Or we can try pumping. You're all exhausted and need some sleep.'

I resist the urge to punch the air in celebration. Someone has finally given me permission to do what I knew was best for my baby and me in the first place. The feeling that I must be able to do everything on my own suffocated me during pregnancy. Before I'd gotten pregnant, Paul and I had agreed that bottle feeding would be best for us all, but the pressure squeezed and squeezed until I felt that I must try to breastfeed Mabli in order to be a proper mum. I stopped trusting myself because I feared I wasn't good enough.

Breastfeeding, I was told over and over in books, by midwives, other mums-to-be and social media would help me bond with Mabli, but it hasn't. It has pushed me closer and closer to the edge, putting distance between us.

The first bottle feed is bliss. That ecstasy I felt when Mabli was first born returns. It's like my brain can't believe that this teeny weensy baby that looks just like me is feeding from a bottle. No longer a hoped-for possibility, but a real baby. I want to shout to the world, *have you seen this magical thing? This baby was grown inside my body and now I'm feeding her. And I've changed her nappy. And burped her. And comforted her when she cried. I've done it all.*

Two weeks after we return home from our extended stay in hospital, Mabli has her first bath. I've put it off for as long as possible because I wanted to give her healthy, glowing skin the best chance possible in adjusting to life outside the womb in our artificially-heated house. I'm excited to see how she responds to water. I'm finally getting to do all the things I'd rehearsed a hundred times in my head, trying to anticipate any potential problems. I'd rather face my fear – and pregnancy had been nine months of compiling lists of my inadequacies.

I'd researched and researched in order to be the perfect mum. After so much reading, listening and watching, my pattern-searching brain noticed one common denominator: no Disabled parents. At least not visibly Disabled parents. Even the big book of everything baby I was given at my twelve-week scan assumed you had a non-disabled body.

Once the bath has filled up, and I've double-checked the temperature, I retrieve the bright orange fox hooded towel we'd bought for her. Paul gently removes all her clothes.

'You better put her in... just in case,' I say. My confidence has been growing, but it's still a seedling.

As soon as her precious little feet touch the water her eyes show alarm. She is aware of a new sensation and she doesn't know whether she is safe. She wriggles in panic. I put my hand on her. Look her straight in the eyes and smile. 'It's ok, Mabli, you're safe. This is going to be a nice, warm bath.' Her body relaxes. She decides not to cry.

'Did you see that?' I say to Paul, stunned.

He nods and smiles. Validation. This perfect baby girl, so vulnerable and yet she trusts me. She believes I have everything I need to keep her safe, even with my Disabled body and addled brain. The wounds of internalised ableism begin to scab over.

*　*　*

A few more weeks pass. We're sharing bottle feeding, everyone is taking turns getting rest and we seem to be hitting our stride, despite the nagging doubts that still stalk me. We've made it out for coffee and to the park. We proudly show Mabli off to strangers and they tell us we're doing so well to be out of the house already. Perhaps I'm not just adequate ... could I be good at this?

This was not what I had expected at all. I'm embarrassed, playing the long reel of memories, all the times I'd cried to various people about how I would not cope, could not be a mum. And they would reassure me and tell me I would do it when the time came. I was certain they were being kind or confusing me for a non-disabled person. Yes, lots of women can do this but I was adamant that *I* couldn't do this. Not with my wonky brain and broken body. I had made a terrible mistake and this innocent baby was going to pay the price for it. They should have mentioned how my non-typical mind and body would make me a better mum. That living with chronic illness is a bootcamp for parenting.

Just as we're planning our first day trip to my favourite beach, a place of refuge and joy I'm excited to share with Mabli, a curveball catches me out. Mabli cries whenever we try to put her down. Not just a 'pick me up' kind of a cry, but a pain cry that sends white-hot fear through my blood. Our happy baby that we had to wake up every four hours will now only sleep when one of us is holding her. Accepting that babies go through phases, we start a shift rotation, which is punishing but it won't be forever, we tell ourselves. Plus I've had plenty of sleepless nights in the past, at least this time I'm cuddling my baby.

After a few feeds – was it days or hours? My sleep-deprived brain has no idea – I notice that it's something to do with her feeding. She used to gulp her milk down enthusiastically. Now she's crying through every feed, arching her back in pain, away from the vexing bottle. The health visitor confirms my suspicions. 'Reflux.'

So off we go to the doctor. Return with milk thickener. A few more feeds pass. An old hand at pain, my empathy sustains me as I soothe her with gentle strokes and whisper encouragements. Her butter-soft skin is now dry and angry red. My detail-oriented mind logs all the ways that Mabli's behaviour and appearance have changed until it establishes the pattern.

'I'm pretty sure she's intolerant to dairy,' I tell Paul after he appears for his shift holding Mabli. She won't let us put her down at all.

'Maybe, we'll see... we could ask the doctor... I don't know.' He's too tired to think clearly. He's worried, exhausted and wants his baby girl to be happy and thriving again.

As I sit a few days later, waiting to see the doctor for the umpteenth time in as many days, my resolve hardens. The professionals have had several attempts at treating Mabli with different medications and formulas, and she's just getting worse. I've done my research and I've watched my baby. I know. There is no way I'm coming away from this appointment without dairy-free formula.

'She improved with the last formula. But she's still not right. She's completely changed. I want to try her on the dairy-free formula.'

'Well you know she is little, you need to manage your expectations around sleep...'

'I'm not concerned by how much we sleep,' I cut the doctor off, 'I'm concerned that she is in pain, not getting adequate sleep, losing weight and showing signs of an allergy. This could all affect her development. What would be the downside?'

The doctor thinks I'm over-the-top; I recognise those pursed lips from many of my own appointments when doctors have been certain that whatever symptom I was complaining about was all in my head. It absolutely could not be the illness I was asking to be tested for, they would say, and yet would go on to be diagnosed with in time.

After looking at her notes on the computer screen, she turns back to us, hands calmly in her lap, ready to begin her speech about why I am wrong. I take deep breaths, trying to mask my emotions. She already thinks I'm irrational – I don't need to give her any more ammo.

'However,' the doctor continues, 'I can see you're concerned so I'll give her a few tins of the dairy-free formula and then you can speak to the dietician next week.' She can't resist adding, 'I doubt she'll be on it for long.'

With one feed Mabli improves. Within a few days she's back on her sleeping schedule, no longer crying through feeds and getting back on target with her weight. Her skin is returning to its alabaster hue. My instinct was right. For the first time I trusted myself and as a result my daughter is getting the treatment she needs.

People queued up to warn me, both before and during pregnancy, that having a child would turn our lives upside down. But amongst the gleeful promises of sleepless nights and obituaries to free time, they didn't tell me how well being Disabled had prepared me. They didn't tell me adapting to a perpetually developing baby was easier than adapting with my dynamic disabilities. They didn't tell me about the healing being a mum would bring.

Biographies / Bywgraffiadau

CAITLIN TINA JONES

Caitlin Tina Jones is an emerging autistic poet from Hengoed, South Wales. Her poems have featured in publications by Pan Macmillan, Propel and Lucent Dreaming, and her poetry reviews have featured in publications by the Institute of Welsh Affairs.

JOSHUA JONES

Joshua Jones (he/him) is a queer, neurodivergent writer from Llanelli, south Wales. *Local Fires* was shortlisted for the Dylan Thomas Prize & Polari First Book Prize. His latest poetry pamphlets are *Three Months in the Zebra Room* (Hello America Stereo Cassette, 2024), and *The City on Film* (Bread and Roses, 2024).

SIONED ERIN HUGHES

Mae Erin yn awdur, ymarferydd creadigol a golygydd Cymraeg, sy'n barddoni weithiau ac yn gweithio fel cydlynydd i'r Gymdeithas Gerdd Dafod, Barddas. Mae wedi ysgrifennu tri llyfr – *Y Goeden Hud* (Gwasg Carreg Gwalch, 2020), *Rhyngom* (Y Lolfa, 2022), ac *O'r Rhuddin* (Y Lolfa, 2024).

KAITE O'REILLY

Kaite O'Reilly is a multi-award-winning playwright and dramaturg, who writes for radio, screen and live performance.

ED GARLAND

Ed Garland's stories have appeared in *The Stinging Fly*, and his essays in the *New Welsh Reader*, *Aural Diversity*, and *Venue Stories*. He is writing his first novel with support from Literature Wales. His website is edgarland.co.uk

BETHANY HANDLEY

Bethany Handley is an award-winning writer, poet and disability activist. Her work has been published in *POETRY*, *Poetry Wales* and *Country Living*, and featured by the Poetry Foundation, BBC Radio 4 and BBC Wales, amongst others. Bethany was awarded Creative Future's Gold Prize for Creative Non-fiction 2023, was shortlisted for the Royal Society of Literature's Jerwood Poetry Prize 2024, and was named in the Shaw Trust's Disability Power 100 2024. *Cling Film*, her debut poetry chapbook, will be published by Seren in February 2025.

J. BELI FRIEL

Beli writes about the intersections of queerness, fatness, disability and class. They are currently working on their first novel. When not writing, they are performing, organising, and dreaming of something better for all of us.

MAGGIE HAMPTON

Maggie is a writer and poet living in south Wales; she often writes about her experiences as a profoundly deaf woman. Her online poetry project 'A Deaf Life' can be seen on www.maggiehampton.co.uk

IESTYN TYNE

Magwyd Iestyn Tyne (fo/ei) yn Llŷn ond mae bellach yn byw yn Waunfawr gyda'i deulu ac yn gweithio yn ardal Caernarfon. Ei gasgliad diweddaraf o farddoniaeth yw *Dysgu Nofio* (Cyhoeddiadau'r Stamp 2023); cyhoeddir *Y Cyfan a fu Rhyngom ni* gan Wasg y Bwthyn yn 2025 ac mae'n un o Gymrodorion Cymru'r Dyfodol 2023–25.

FRAN KIRCHHOLTES

Fran Kirchholtes is a neurodivergent writer and stage manager living in South Wales. Originally from Germany, she graduated from Royal Welsh College of Music and Drama and has been working in theatre ever since. Writing prose, poetry and drama is Fran's preferred method of expressing herself.

LEIGH MANLEY

Leigh Manley is a working-class poet and creative facilitator from Maesteg. He turned to writing for therapeutic reasons after being diagnosed with arrhythmogenic cardiomyopathy and experiencing unexpected ableist judgements. His work aims to educate others on the complexity of invisible illness.

GREG GLOVER

Greg is an award-winning writer who has written for radio and television. He's had his work performed on stages that include The Sherman and Bristol Old Vic. He was recently chosen by Theatr Iolo as one of their Platfform artists.

SARA ERDDIG

Sara Louise Wheeler writes the columns "O'r gororau" (Barddas) and "Synfyfyrion Sara" (Golwg360). "Ablaeth Rhemp y Crachach" won Disability Arts Cymru's 2022 'Creative Words' award (Welsh-medium). *Trawiad | Seizure* (2023) and *A Goareig Patchwork Quilt* (2024) are her latest chapbooks.

JAMIE WOODS

Jamie Woods is a writer from Swansea, with work published in *iamb*, *Acropolis*, *Poetry Wales* and more. Poet-in-residence at Leukaemia Care, his pamphlet *Rebel Blood Cells* (Punk Dust Poetry) deals with the impact of cancer and PTSD. www.jamiewoods77.com

KATHERINE WILLIAMS

Katherine Williams writes about identity, experience and music. She grew up in Wales and Shropshire, and now lives in Bristol with her husband and two children.

LENI FRANK

Leni is an autistic writer from Eryri, Wales who lives in a chaotic home with two teenagers, a tyrannous cat and a timid dog. Keen, but quiet member of local writing group.

GUINEVERE CLARK

Guinevere Clark: PhD in Creative Writing and Founder of Poetry Into Light. She's published widely: *Poetry Wales*, *Atlanta Review*, *Magma* and beyond, is a co-editor with the feminist journal Demeter Press and teaches poetry at Swansea's Taliesin Arts Centre. www.poetryintolight.org

LUCY AUR

A Welsh writer with a recently earned PhD in Creative Writing. Published poet and short story writer including 'Heaven is a Coffee Shop' which debuted in 2023. Lucy is a passionate mental health campaigner and avid volunteer, founder of Renegades Foundation and advocate for Welsh representation in the arts.

REBECCA WILSON

Rebecca Wilson is a Welsh and Jewish writer originally from Eryri. Her children's picture book *The Winter Festival* was published by Rily in October 2024. She has also written under commission for Theatr Clwyd, Young Pleasance, Theatr Genedlaethol Cymru and Sherman Theatre. Her essay 'Tikkun Olam: Stitching together Welsh and Jewish identities' was published in *The Welsh Agenda*, 2023.

FREYA F. ELLIOTT

Freya F. Elliott – stylised as f.f. elliott – is a lesbian writer and poet based in South Wales. She aims to combine environmental imagery of the natural world with themes such as queer love and friendship, gender identity and expression, and grief and trauma. She is also partially Deaf and currently seeking a diagnosis for Autism.

SIÂN ROBERTS
Un o Bencader, Sir Gaerfyrddin yw Siân ond mae'n byw yn Nhrefor, Caernarfon, ers dros 40 mlynedd. Mae'n gyfieithydd ar ei liwt ei hun. Cafodd ddiagnosis o MS yn 2014 ond mae'n dal i fwynhau bywyd.

SAM SKELTON
Amongst other academic achievements, Sam Skelton held a Creative Writing Masters from Cardiff Met and was on the UniSlam 2021 winning team. She was trained in theatre and was an active member of Bristol's 'Kelvin Players' winning awards for both directing and acting. She was an actor and teacher and now a published writer. She lived in Caerleon and passed away from metastatic lung cancer and is survived by her husband, sister, mother, three children, two step-children and beloved dog.

MATTHEW HAIGH
Matthew Haigh is the author of *Death Magazine* (Salt), *Vampires* (Bad Betty) and *Black Jam* (Broken Sleep Books). He was nominated for the Polari First Book Prize and the Michael Marks Award. He lives in Cardiff.

DEE MONTAGUE
Dee Montague (she/her) lives in Newport with her husband and stepdaughter. She spends most of her time in her bedroom hanging out with her feline colleagues, Ahsoka and Bo-Catan. A proudly queer Disabled demiwoman, Dee is passionate about intersectional female health equity.

PAUL DAVIES
Paul left behind a successful career as a broadcast journalist and producer to spend more time with his mental illness. He can be found avoiding responsibility in the Welsh mountains or by searching @p_m_davies wherever you do your doom scrolling.

DIFFWYS CRIAFOL
Diffwys Criafol is the pen name of an activist turned writer, interested in distilling the lessons of 15 years of political activity while finding herself in a slew of marginalised life contexts. Her work encompasses anarchist & prison abolitionist ideas, along the intersections of class, gender, language & disability.

RACHEL CARNEY
Rachel Carney is a creative writing tutor based in Cardiff. Her debut poetry collection *Octopus Mind* was selected as one of *The Guardian's* Best Poetry Books of 2023 and is published by Seren Books.

LEE GREEN
Lee Green is a neurodivergent queer writer and artist from North Wales who is passionate about disability accessibility and working towards societal shifts in perspective regarding Disabled people.

SOFIA BRIZIO

Sofia Brizio is an Italian writer, translator and editor based in Wales. Living with cerebral palsy, Sofia writes about disability rights, LGBTQ+ rights, and trans-inclusive intersectional feminism. She is currently a PhD researcher in Media Diversity at Birmingham City University.

ZOË BRIGLEY

Zoë Brigley has three poetry collections published by Bloodaxe, most recently *Hand & Skull*. All three were PBS Recommendations as well as winning an Eric Gregory Award, being longlisted for the Dylan Thomas Prize and Forward Prize commended.

KATIE BENNETT DAVIES

After running out of excuses not to write, Katie decided the only option left was to become a mother. She lives (mostly) horizontally, alongside her cat, daughter, husband, and vast conker collection. You can find her on Instagram @teambdinandout

Acknowledgements / Cydnabyddiaethau

Mae'n rhaid i ni ddiolch o waelod calon i staff Llenyddiaeth Cymru a Thŷ Newydd am eu cefnogaeth ddiflino dros y ddwy flynedd ddiwethaf. Ni fyddai'r flodeugerdd hon yn bodoli oni bai am eu nawdd, ar y cyd â nawdd Cyfoeth Naturiol Cymru yn ôl yn 2022 a alluogodd i Beth a Megan gynnal cwrs ysgrifennu creadigol ar gyfer awduron Byddar ac a/Anabl yn Nhŷ Newydd. Y cwrs hwn sbardunodd y syniad ar gyfer y flodeugerdd hon. At hynny, roedd y tair ohonom yn rhan o garfan Cynrychioli Cymru 2023–24. Mae'r rhaglen hon wedi chwarae rhan allweddol yn ein datblygiad fel awduron, ac wedi ein harfogi gydag addysg ddihafal wrth fynd ati i ysgrifennu am faterion o bwys.

Meanwhile the beautiful Tŷ Newydd gave us a rarely accessible place to discuss this anthology, where the usual barriers we experience were removed. Mae ein gwerthfawrogiad yn enfawr.

Jannat and the Lucent Dreaming team; we cannot thank you enough for your faith and unwavering support of this anthology from the very beginning, when it was just a seed of an idea. Thank you for your trust in us, for your invaluable advice and expertise and for your tireless work in ensuring that the Welsh literature landscape is as diverse and vivid as its population.

I'r holl gyfranwyr ac i'r holl sgwenwyr talentog a gyflwynodd eu gwaith i'r alwad agored, diolch am rannu eich straeon mor hael gyda ni'n tair. Maen nhw'n straeon sydd angen eu hadrodd a'u clywed yn eang, ac rydyn ni'n teimlo'n freintiedig tu hwnt ein bod ni ymhlith y llygaid cyntaf i ddarllen eich gwaith. Diolch am eich bregusrwydd, eich gonestrwydd a'ch angerdd, a diolch hefyd am eich amynedd wrth i'r broses o dynnu'r flodeugerdd ynghyd fynd rhagddi.

To all the contributors and to all the talented writers who submitted, thank you for generously sharing your work with us. These are stories that need to be told and heard, and we feel extremely privileged to be among the first eyes to read your work. Thank you for your vulnerability, your honesty and your passion, and thank you for your patience while we pieced together this anthology.

Mae ein diolch yn enfawr i'r artist arbennig Cerys Knighton am ei harlunwaith eithriadol o dlws a chain ar gyfer y clawr. Ni fyddwn wedi gallu dychmygu darlun mwy trawiadol nac addas i gynrychioli'r flodeugerdd.

Diolch yn fawr iawn to Books Council of Wales for their New Audiences fund which seeks to represent Wales in all its diversity and has enabled us to create a space for, and preserve, some of the rich and diverse voices of contemporary Wales for future generations to come.

Diolch i'n teulu, ein ffrindiau a'n cymuned am eu chwilfrydedd yn ein gwaith, eu gofal a'u hanogaeth gyson wrth i ni gyflawni'r flodeugerdd.

Thank you to our family, friends and community for their curiosity in our work and their constant care and encouragement as we nurtured this anthology.

The final thanks goes to the Deaf and Disabled communities and to all the Deaf and Disabled writers and activists who have come before, paving the way. The creativity, resilience and generosity of our communities is invaluable to us.

Mae creadigrwydd, gwytnwch a haelioni ein cymunedau wironeddol werth y byd.